SHAPING
HIGHER
EDUCATION'S
FUTURE

*Arthur Levine
and Associates*

SHAPING HIGHER EDUCATION'S FUTURE

Demographic Realities and Opportunities, 1990–2000

 Jossey-Bass Publishers

San Francisco • Oxford • 1990

SHAPING HIGHER EDUCATION'S FUTURE
Demographic Realities and Opportunities, 1990-2000
by Arthur Levine and Associates

Copyright © 1989 by: Jossey-Bass Inc., Publishers
350 Sansome Street
San Francisco, California 94104
&
Jossey-Bass Limited
Headington Hill Hall
Oxford OX3 0BW

Library of Congress Cataloging-in-Publication Data

Shaping higher education's future : demographic realities and
  opportunities, 1990-2000 / Arthur Levine and associates. — 1st ed.
      p.   cm. — (The Jossey-Bass higher education series)
  Includes bibliographical references.
  ISBN 1-55542-191-1
  1. Education, Higher — United States — Forecasting — Congresses.
  2. Education — Demographic aspects — United States — Congresses.
  I. Levine, Arthur.   II. Series.
  LA227.3.S47   1989
  378.73'09'049 — dc20   89-45576
                                                                          CIP

Manufactured in the United States of America

The paper in this book meets the guidelines for
permanence and durability of the Committee on
Production Guidelines for Book Longevity of
the Council on Library Resources.

JACKET DESIGN BY WILLI BAUM

FIRST EDITION
    First printing: November 1989
    Second printing: July 1990

Code 8963

The Jossey-Bass
Higher Education Series

Table of

Contents

cont.

Chap.

Chap.

Chap.

E/O T3C

Preface

This book stems from a symposium on the demographics of
American higher education sponsored by the Ford Foundation.
The premise of this symposium was that the world of higher
education is changing dramatically. Our nation is increasingly
becoming part of a global society. Our economy is moving from
an industrial to an information and service base. Our population is undergoing a demographic metamorphosis. New technol-
ogies are burgeoning. Our social institutions — family, schools,
media — are being transformed. The era of New Deal politics is
waning. In the past few years, the accent has been on shrinking
the size and influence of the federal government. Social programs,
including education initiatives, have diminished in priority.

As a consequence, many elements of higher education are
in flux. The demographic profile of our students and potential
students is changing. The relationship between higher education
and the federal government, state governments, industry, and
other external patrons is shifting. The financing of colleges and
universities is undergoing a change. Critical research on learning is multiplying, and experiments applying this research to
instruction, particularly in the business world, are mushrooming.

The modern American system of higher education came
of age in the years following World War II. It was rooted in
the premise of growth — increasing resources and rising numbers
of students. But more than this, it was grounded in a postwar
social, economic, technological, political, and even demographic
vision of America. Now we have reached a turning point. The
era of growth is past, and the postwar assumptions about the
nation are no longer accurate.

These new realities are going to require new responses from higher education. Old answers will not work as well as they once did. We are already seeing discrepancies. As the role of the federal government begins to decline in favor of the states, the response of higher education's spokespeople has been that Washington should reembrace its old role as higher education's greatest patron. To reductions in financial aid, higher education's only response has been to ask the government to restore past funding levels. To the questions that have been raised about the state of undergraduate education, the only answers have been the tired ones that we have heard over and over again. We have reached a point at which the solutions offered to higher education's pressing problems are all too familiar and less helpful than they once were.

The Ford Foundation's symposium on demographics was intended to reexamine one of the areas of most profound change for higher education. For a decade and a half, a raft of demographic publications and projections have attempted to chart the future of America's colleges and universities. Unfortunately, they have not been particularly successful in their predictions or in their explication.

The symposium, which was a full-day colloquium, attempted to fill this gap. Five papers were commissioned in preparation for it. They analyzed higher education's key populations — eighteen-year-olds, adults, blacks, Hispanics, and Asians. Using these papers as a starting point, participants in the symposium considered the nation's most probable demographic future. They focused on areas of agreement and disagreement, both of which were many; the implications of potential demographic changes for higher education; useful responses by colleges and publics (government, foundations, the schools); and the limits of demographic thinking and projections.

Participating in the discussions were Alison Bernstein (Ford Foundation), William F. Brazziel (University of Connecticut), Helen Cunningham (Pew Memorial Trust), Richard A. Easterlin (University of Southern California), Carol Frances (Carol Frances and Associates), Barbara Hatton (Ford Foundation), Harold Hodgkinson (American Council on Education), Arthur Levine (then at Bradford College), Gary Orfield (University of Chicago), Lewis C. Solmon (University of California, Los Angeles), Peter Stanley (Ford Foundation), Bob H. Suzuki (California State University, Northridge), and Gail Thomas (Texas A&M University).

Shaping Higher Education's Future, a product of the symposium, analyzes the needs and future of higher education's key populations, discusses the limits of demographic analysis and projection, offers a set of conclusions about future demographic trends, and recommends ways that higher education can respond to them. The conclusions and recommendations grew out of the discussions at the symposium and do not reflect the opinion of any one individual.

This book differs in several respects from what has previously been written about the demographics of higher education. First, the authors seek to minimize the emphasis on long-term projection, focusing instead on the years 1989 to 2000 — that is, on the short term. Thus, all the people who will be attending college during this period have already been born. Their numbers can be counted rather than guessed at.

Second, the book is comprehensive. Various chapters examine each of the five major groups that might potentially have the largest impact on higher education during the remainder of this century: traditional college-age students (eighteen years of age), adults, blacks, Asians, and Hispanics. Each chapter considers the history of a particular group; its changing population realities with respect to size, location, and social conditions; the quality of available data on the group; past and likely future educational expectancies for the group, along with factors that could change those expectations; and the implications for higher education. The goal here has been to avoid the problems that too often plague writing on demographics in higher education — a focus on the nation as a whole rather than on the subgroups that compose it; an emphasis on an ethnic or racial group as a whole rather than on the subpopulations it includes; acceptance of available data without explanation of their weaknesses; and advocacy for a particular group rather than analysis of its actual situation.

Third, the authorship is unique. The chapters are written by scholars who have achieved a reputation for studying particular populations rather than by students of higher education who have an interest in demography. We hope this perspective will enable us to improve on higher education policymakers and researchers' track record in projecting enrollments.

Fourth, this volume considers both the limits of demographic data and the possible alternative futures for higher education. Nationally known scholars have been asked to place the data on traditional-age, adult, black, Asian, and Hispanic students in perspective to point out the potential holes and weaknesses in demographic theory.

Overview of the Contents

Shaping Higher Education's Future is divided into two parts. Part One, which deals with coming demographic changes in higher education, begins with an introductory chapter by Arthur Levine, which describes the demographic landscape of the nation. Chapter Two, by Lewis C. Solmon, focuses on traditional-age college students, Chapter Three, by Gary Orfield, on Hispanic students, Chapter Four, by Gail E. Thomas and Deborah J. Hirsch, on black students, Chapter Five, by Bob H. Suzuki, on Asian students, and Chapter Six, by William F. Brazziel, on adult students.

Part Two, in which we consider the limits of demographics, contains two chapters: Chapter Seven, by Richard A. Easterlin, looks at factors beyond population figures that can change attendance rates at colleges and universities, while Chapter Eight, by Carol Frances, focuses on the appropriate use of demographic data, as well as on the kinds of data misuse that have hindered higher education enrollment planning.

In Chapter Nine, Arthur Levine draws together the findings of the other authors about the demographic future of higher education and suggests ways that colleges and universities can shape demographic realities to create a brighter future. It is a record of the conclusions reached by the participants in the Ford Foundation symposium.

Audience

This volume is intended for college administrators — for presidents as well as for academic, administrative, student affairs, and admissions officers, all of whom must take the lead in educating the changing populations of the years ahead. It is intended for the faculty members who will teach future student generations — and for policymakers: trustees, state and federal higher education leaders, and education association staffers.

Acknowledgments

I thank the Ford Foundation and particularly Peter Stanley for making the symposium and this book possible. My thanks go also to each of the participants in the symposium for making it successful and for contributing to *Shaping Higher Education's Future*. And I thank Deborah J. Hirsch, Eileen Welch, and Claire Wilson at Bradford College for their prodigious efforts in organizing the symposium and for their work with the authors and manuscripts.

Signed
(SP)
Arthur Levine

Cambridge, Massachusetts
September 1989

E/o Preface

p. XVI Contains Dedication
which has been lead

Dedication

**To my good friends and teachers
JB and Earline Hefferlin**

c/o Dedication

About

The Authors

Arthur Levine is chairman of the Institute of Educational Management and a member of the senior faculty of the Harvard Graduate School of Education. From 1982 to 1989, he was president of Bradford College. Before going to Bradford, Levine served as Senior Fellow at the Carnegie Foundation for the Advancement of Teaching in Washington, D.C., and at the Carnegie Council on Policy Studies in Higher Education in Berkeley, California.

Levine received his B.A. degree (1970) from Brandeis University in biology. He earned his Ph.D. degree (1976) from the State University of New York, Buffalo, in the fields of sociology and higher education.

Levine is the author of dozens of articles and reviews. *Opportunity in Adversity,* which he coedited with Janice Green, was published in 1985. His other books include *Handbook on Undergraduate Curriculum* (1979), *When Dreams and Heroes Died: A Portrait of Today's College Students* (1980), *Why Innovation Fails* (1980), and *Quest for Common Learning* (1981, with E. Boyer). A 1982 Guggenheim Fellowship holder, Levine has also been awarded the American Council on Education Book of the Year Award for *Reform of Undergraduate Education* (1973), the Education Press Association of America's award for best article (1981 and 1989), and honorary degrees from five institutions. He has served as consultant to more than 150 colleges and universities.

William F. Brazziel is professor of higher education and director of graduate programs in higher education at the University of Connecticut. He received both his B.S. degree (1948) from Central State University of Ohio and his M.S. degree

(1949) from Pennsylvania State University in biochemistry, and his Ph.D. degree (1956) from Ohio State University in higher education and administration.

Brazziel was a member of Connecticut's first Higher Education Master Plan Commission. He has served as a member of the National Advisory Committee on Education Professions. He has also served as director of the National Leadership Training Institute, a research and dissemination center of the U.S. Office of Education.

Brazziel is author of *Quality Education for All Americans* (1974). He is coauthor of *Higher Education for All Americans* (1983, with M. Brazziel). In 1964, he completed the first research project of the newly created Office of Manpower and Automation. The study examined workers' decisions to retrain in the face of possible displacement in increasingly automated and computerized workplaces. The resulting research monograph, *Workers' Decisions to Retrain* (1964), informs federal policy today. Recently, Brazziel's article "Waiting for the Older Student" (1985) was read into the *Congressional Record* and was referred to on the floor of the U.S. House of Representatives as the "single piece which best encapsulates the changes colleges and universities must make to accommodate the lifelong learners now coming to their campuses."

Richard A. Easterlin is professor of economics at the University of Southern California, Los Angeles. From 1948 to 1982, he taught at the University of Pennsylvania, where he served four times as chair of the Department of Economics.

He received his M.E. degree (1945) from the Stevens Institute of Technology in engineering and both his A.M. (1949) and Ph.D. (1953) degrees from the University of Pennsylvania in economics.

His publications include *Birth and Fortune: The Impact of Numbers on Personal Welfare* (2nd ed., 1987), *The Fertility Revolution: A Supply-Demand Analysis* (1985, with E. M. Crimmins), *Population, Labor Force, and Long Swings in Economic Growth: The American Experience* (1968), and *Population Redistribution and Economic Growth, United States, 1890–1950* (2nd ed. 1960, with others).

He is currently a Fellow of the Guggenheim Foundation and has been a Fellow of the Econometric Society (1983) and of the American Academy of Arts and Sciences (1978). He has served as the president of both the Population Association of America (1978) and the Economic History Association (1979–80).

Carol Frances is a specialist in the economics and finance of higher education. She works with Washington-based education associations, individual colleges and universities, businesses, and government agencies. She is economic and program adviser to the Association of Urban Universities. She is also a partner in Performance, a firm specializing in strategic planning. She has been asked to testify on education finance issues before congressional committees.

Frances received a B.A. degree from the University of California, Los Angeles, and a second undergraduate degree from the Institut d'Etudes Politiques in Paris, both in international relations; master's degrees from Stanford University and Yale University; and a Ph.D. degree from Duke University in economics. She serves as vice-chair of the board of trustees of Southeastern University.

Deborah J. Hirsch is assistant to the president at Bradford College and a doctoral candidate at Harvard University's Graduate School of Education. She received her B.S. degree (1984) from Boston University in special education and elementary education, and M.Ed. degrees from the State University of New York, Buffalo (1984), and the Harvard Graduate School of Education (1986).

Gary Orfield is professor of political science and education at the University of Chicago. He directed the Metropolitan Opportunity Project, a study of changing patterns in education, job training, and employment in five of the largest metropolitan areas in the United States.

Orfield received his B.A. degree (1963) from the University of Minnesota and both his M.A. degree (1965) and his

Ph.D. degree (1968) from the University of Chicago in political science.

Lewis C. Solmon is dean of the UCLA Graduate School of Education. His current research focuses on merit pay, the costs and benefits of having foreign students in American universities, and issues in elementary and secondary school reform. As president of Human Resources Policy Corporation (from 1979 to the present), Solmon provides economic analysis for private business and industry.

Before coming to UCLA, Solmon served from 1972 to 1974 as staff director for the National Research Council's Commission on Human Resources, based in Washington, D.C., was an assistant professor of economics at the City University of New York and Purdue University, and held a research fellowship at the National Bureau of Economic Research. *Change* magazine voted him one of 100 top young leaders in the American Academy in 1978. He has served as an adviser to the World Bank, UNESCO, the American Educational Research Association, the American Council on Education, and the National Endowment for the Humanities.

Solmon received his B.Com. degree (1964) from the University of Toronto and his A.M. degree (1967) and Ph.D. degree (1968) from the University of Chicago, all in economics. He has written more than twenty books and monographs and fifty articles. His textbook, *Economics,* which is currently in its third edition, is used by college students nationwide.

Bob H. Suzuki is vice-president for academic affairs and professor of social and philosophical foundations at California State University, Northridge. He is the author of many articles on Asian Americans and education and a specialist in the fields of multicultural and international education.

In addition to his scholarly pursuits, he has been active for more than two decades in the areas of civil and human rights and in 1976 was the first recipient of the National Education Association's Human Rights Award for Leadership in Asian and Pacific Island Affairs.

He received his B.S. (1960) and M.S. (1962) degrees from the University of California, Berkeley, in mechanical engineering and his Ph.D. degree (1967) from the California Institute of Technology in aeronautics.

Gail E. Thomas is professor of sociology at Texas A&M University. Her main research interests are the educational attainment of underrepresented minorities and stratification and inequality.

She is currently conducting a national study of institutions that grant doctoral degrees to investigate their policies and practices in recruiting, enrolling, and retaining U.S. black and Hispanic students. She is also working at present on an edited volume on American race relations.

Thomas has served on various national committees and task forces aimed at reducing educational and social inequality and enhancing educational progress and opportunities for underrepresented minorities. She has published extensively in social science and higher education journals.

SHAPING HIGHER EDUCATION'S FUTURE

1

Introduction: A Time of Uncertainty

Arthur Levine

Snapshot

Not long ago I visited the neighborhood where I grew up. My old neighborhood was a place of dreams—large dreams, grand dreams. And for the most part those dreams were both fulfillable and fulfilled. My friends and I went to college, even though many of our parents had not even finished high school. Today, Barry and Jimmy are teachers, Debby is a nurse, Elliot staffs a federal program, Marvin and Eddie are doctors, and Steven is a Wall Street investor. On my block the American dream flourished. In fact, it was virtually guaranteed.

The apartment building I grew up in still stands today, a little over two decades since I left to go to college. But the people who live there are different. They are poor, no longer working class. They are Hispanic and black, no longer white.

When I lived there in 1960, the average family income was $5,600. In 1980, the most recent year for census data, it was $4,900. In 1960, the unemployment rate was 6 percent. In 1980, it was 38 percent, and nearly three out of five men were unemployed. In 1960, 85 percent of all youngsters under eighteen lived with both parents. In 1980, 71 percent lived with a female head of household.

1

Today, only a third of the adults are high school graduates. The dominant source of income is public assistance. A majority of residents move out of the neighborhood every five years. Drug problems, teenage pregnancies, and school dropout rates are soaring.

Walk through the neighborhood today and see mounds of rubble and garbage where buildings once stood. See basements piled thigh high with rubbish.

Walk into my old building. See the pried-open mailboxes, few of which have names. See the man passed out on the stairs between the third and fourth floors.

Meet the residents of my old neighborhood. I am told they include a thirteen-year-old mother of two, a twenty-six-year-old grandmother, and a twelve-year-old junkie.

But the saddest part of my old neighborhood is that the dreams are gone. It's the same piece of real estate—the same building. But the hope, the promise, and the opportunity associated with education have disappeared. Just talk to the kids. They will tell you.

Snapshot

Near the community where I currently live is the city of Lawrence, Massachusetts. Once it was home to an assortment of European immigrant groups. Today, it has an ever increasing Hispanic and Asian population. I spent a week living in a low-income project there.

I talked with the children, scores of them, of elementary and junior high school age. I asked them what they wanted to be when they grew up. The answers were what one would expect—teacher, secretary, policeman, fireman, carpenter. I asked the kids whether they thought they would have a chance to do these things—the response was usually a no or a shrug.

We talked about education, and I asked them what was the furthest they could imagine going in school. The most common answer was 10th grade, followed by 12th. The highest aspiration for most of these children was to be a high school dropout. They didn't know anyone who had been to college.

In fact, the people the children knew who had finished high school were distant connections — a mother's cousin, a sister's date.

Drugs came up in most conversations. Drugs are a taken-for-granted reality in the lives of these children. A nine-year-old casually told me, "My mother's friend took too many drugs. She and her baby died." Only one of the kids I talked with told me that he did not know where to buy drugs. And I didn't believe him.

The kids of Lawrence see a real and seamy side of life early. In a two-hour stroll around the neighborhood one day, I saw a drug bust, a group of prostitutes being rousted, a woman hit by a car, and a police frisking. The naiveté and dreams of childhood are not part of life in the project.

The children I met were frequently premature births, had fallen behind grade level in school, had poor diets, lived almost exclusively in female-headed households, had serious language deficiencies, and began having children as children. For them, going to college is not only unlikely; it is incomprehensible.

Snapshot

I was a brand-new college president. I was about to award my first college degree — to a student who had missed commencement because of an illness. As I walked into my waiting room to meet her, I realized this was a very special occasion, more special than I ever imagined. Her grandmother was already there. I chitchatted with the woman while waiting for her granddaughter to arrive. About ten minutes into the conversation, the woman asked if she could have a picture of me handing her diploma to her. My first college degree was given to a seventy-three-year-old woman.

Snapshot

This college is set in the poorest congressional district in the United States. The first thing I saw was a large rat foraging on the main street where the college is located. The institution itself is composed of four buildings on opposite sides of the street in a run-down, partially abandoned residential and commercial district. If you didn't know you were looking for a college on this street, it would be easy to miss.

There are lots of locks and lots of guards at the doors. But inside are students lounging around very comfortably. There are signs in Spanish and English, announcements of events, and messages offering hope and encouragement — *Saber es Poder* (Knowledge is Power).

This is Hostos Community College. It enrolls over 4,800 students. Eighty-seven percent of them are Hispanics. Nearly all live below the poverty line, and almost half (49 percent) have family incomes of less than $4,000. Seventy percent of the students are women. A majority of the students are single heads of households with dependent children.

The average age of Hostos students is twenty-seven. Less than one-tenth of them come directly from high school, and more than a third have general equivalency diplomas.

Hostos, which opened its doors in 1970, has three goals for its students — to provide bilingual education in order to remove language barriers to higher education; to provide career and technical programs that lead to employment and socioeconomic mobility; and to provide knowledge and critical thinking skills for life, senior college transfer, and professional advancement through the liberal arts. The faculty is 40 percent Hispanic, 20 percent black, and 48 percent female. It is a unique institution geared to a distinctive population.

The challenges that Hostos encounters are also unusual. They include a student body that, because it is not proficient in English, requires on average a minimum of four years of full-time study to complete an associate degree. There is little cultural or family support for its students, particularly for its female students. Child care and public school hours constrict attendance. State and federal financial aid does not adequately support the remediation that its students need. Traditional student recruiting practices don't work. In short, Hostos is a very different kind of college with some very different kinds of problems.

Snapshot

Like Hostos, it is a community college. Like Hostos, it is located in a poor minority neighborhood. And like Hostos, it enrolls about 5,000 predominantly minority students with comparable skills and abilities.

But the similarities end there. This community college was created in the late 1950s for students who lacked the grades to enter the highly selective public university. By the mid 1960s, it was enrolling a predominantly white student body that graduated from its secondary school classes with *B* averages. This community college thought of itself as the Harvard of two-year schools. But then, in less than a decade, the neighborhood changed dramatically.

The college never adapted to its new students. Though its facilities are far more attractive than those of Hostos, the warmth is lacking. The institution seems large, formal, and distant. Students do not "hang around" the campus. Many faculty hold their students in disdain. They resent the loss of the students of the sixties and feel that their talents are being wasted. More and more faculty members are spending less and less time on campus. Student services complain of being understaffed. In contrast to Hostos, few of the staff come from backgrounds similar to those of the students. The messages of encouragement and hope are absent. The two schools could not be more different.

These snapshots reflect the changing demographic landscape of American higher education. This landscape includes new populations — some pouring into college in unprecedented, hitherto unimaginable numbers and others for whom college is virtually unattainable. It includes traditional populations — some well known to be declining, others changing dramatically but in ways as yet unrecognized. It includes new colleges for new students. It includes older institutions with changing populations that are adapting both well and poorly to their new clienteles. And it includes schools that have heard about a demographic revolution but have seen little if any change in their student bodies.

For more than a decade higher education has been sounding the demographic alarm. New populations are coming! New populations are coming! Harold Hodgkinson, higher education's most visible student of demographics, has become a modern-day Paul Revere.

Yet it is difficult to find this demographic revolution. There are some notable exceptions — 1989 was the year in which admissions applications began dropping in colleges and universities in some parts of the country. However, overall, little seems to have changed across American higher education. Despite decreasing numbers of eighteen-year-olds, college enrollments are still up. Despite increasing numbers of minorities, the proportion of blacks and Hispanics in college is down.

The reason is that this is a demographic revolution in which the whole is less than the sum of the parts. It is not for the most part a national phenomenon. It is a story of dramatic changes that vary from region to region of the country. What is happening in the West is not occurring in the east. The North and South differ sharply. Even states that border one another are facing very different demographic realities.

The demographic revolution is a tale of different peoples — rising and falling numbers of older and younger persons; men and women; whites, blacks, Asians, Hispanics, and others. It is a matter of divisions within racial and ethnic groups. Cubans, Dominicans, Puerto Ricans, and Mexican Americans are all Hispanics, but each group has a profoundly different attendance rate in higher education, different eductional needs, and different educational values. Asians can be similarly divided — the Vietnamese resemble Puerto Ricans in educational respects more than they do Chinese or Filipinos. Chinese have higher attendance rates in college than whites. The demographic revolution is also a matter of immigration — where new Americans are coming from, how many are entering the country, and where they are settling down.

The demographic revolution is an account of distinct types of institutions. Two-year colleges, four-year colleges, and universities are feeling the effects of demographic changes in remarkably different ways. Public and private schools vary as well. Then there are the specialized institutions, including the older black colleges, the newer Hispanic schools, and the mix of Native American institutions. In a very real sense the demographic revolution is three thousand separate futures for American colleges and universities.

This chapter began with a series of snapshots. Two stand in stark contrast — Hostos Community College and a second, unnamed two-year school. They educate the same students, but Hostos was created with these students in mind. Hostos faculty and staff embraced these students, and the college designed academic and support programs for them. Hostos geared its schedule, physical plant, and support programs to the needs of these students.

By contrast, at the other college, the population changed by chance. The faculty and staff resented their new students. Programming changed slowly and reluctantly to somewhat better meet student needs. The plant is little used by students outside of class.

As a result, the enrollment at Hostos rose consistently while the other college's enrollment plummeted before finally stabilizing. Morale among Hostos staff is high while the other school is dispirited. The sense of community is strong among Hostos students and largely absent at the other school.

These two colleges illustrate the promise and pitfalls of demographics. Every college has the ability within limits either to actively shape its demographic future as Hostos did or to ignore the changing populations and accept the future that is dealt it. After-the-fact resentment, denial, and withdrawal, as practiced at the unnamed two-year college, will not change the numbers. Thoughtful analysis and creative thinking about tomorrow are far more useful responses.

This book is intended to make sense of the complex demographic future facing higher education. Its aims are two: (1) to assist individual institutions to understand and to respond to the unique conditions facing them and (2) to provide higher education as a whole, the policy implications of the demographic changes ahead.

The chapters that follow present a picture of higher education's many demographic futures and the multiple factors that will shape these futures. They offer an analysis of the limits of demographic thinking, and they present a series of recommendations aimed at helping colleges and universities consciously shape tomorrow rather than having it arrive by accident.

E/o Chap. 1

PART ONE   (no leep)

Demographic Changes Ahead for Higher Education

p. 10 is blank

Traditional College-Age Students

Lewis C. Solmon (SP) (NOTE)

The large and growing number of births during the postwar baby-boom period (1946 to 1964) led to an unprecedented expansion in the American system of higher education seventeen to nineteen years later. Although the number of births began to decline in the late 1950s, the expected commensurate decline in college enrollments approximately eighteen years later was not realized. Even though the rapid growth in the number of eighteen-year-olds ended in the mid 1970s, between that time and approximately 1982 we observed for the most part a relatively flat number of eighteen-year-olds. After 1982, however, the number of eighteen-year-olds began to decline sharply and will continue to do so until the last several years of the 1990s. There is thus no question that college enrollments will decline dramatically between now and the end of the twentieth century.

Birthrates have been the primary predictor of college enrollments approximately eighteen years into the future, but there are a number of reasons why this measure does not translate exactly to college enrollments. The most significant is that the United States has always attracted large numbers of immigrants

Note: The author would like to acknowledge the assistance of Deborah Banks, (SP) who contributed to an earlier version of this chapter. R I T

from other countries. Since the 1970s, this has been a particularly important factor. We have seen immigration from various nations in Asia as a result of military and political upheavals in that part of the world, and from Central and South America because of the economic disadvantages experienced by many citizens in Latin America. In general, as long as the standard of living in the United States remains superior to that in many other parts of the world, there will be a continuing stream of foreigners who seek entry into the United States through either legal or illegal means.

Two other categories of factors have the potential for altering relationships between birthrates and college enrollments. The first of these relates to economics and the labor market. During the early and mid 1970s, some argued that since more and more college graduates were entering the labor market each year because of the increasing number of eighteen-year-olds resulting from the baby boom, the supply of college graduates for the labor force would increase relative to demand for them, while the number of those with less than a college education would decline. It was predicted that this trend would result in a relative scarcity of less skilled workers. This set of circumstances would, moreover, diminish the rate of return from a college education compared to the rate of return from a high school education. Incentives would therefore arise for individuals to enter the labor market rather than attend college (Freeman, 1976; Dresch, 1975).

There is no question that the number of jobs of the type traditionally held by college graduates (prior to the baby boom) did not grow as quickly as the number of college graduates during the 1960s and 1970s. However, the rate of return from a college education (the difference between the earnings of a college graduate and the earnings of a high school graduate adjusted for the incremental costs of attending college, including forgone earnings) has not declined as expected (O'Neill and Sepielli, 1985). As more college graduates entered the labor market, they found themselves taking jobs that previously had been held by those with less than a college education. Employers expanded the scope of these jobs to take advantage of the additional skills and talents of those who now hold them, and the earnings of college graduates remained steady (Solmon and Ochsner, 1979). In addition, unemployment rates have remained much lower for college graduates. These economic considerations, along with the fact that people attend college for reasons in addition to economic ones, served to support the desire for a college education despite the fact that there were so many people with college degrees.

The second set of factors that tend to lessen the correlation between birthrates and subsequent college enrollments involve the standards and behavior of educational institutions at the precollegiate level. Since larger and larger proportions of the college-age cohort were completing high school each year, the proportion of eighteen-year-olds who were eligible for college increased. Moreover, since the system of higher education as a whole and many of the institutions within it had expanded in order to accommodate the growing number of baby boomers, the subsequent decline in absolute numbers of eighteen-year-olds led many institutions to admit greater proportions of the smaller high school classes.

Some institutions expanded to meet the needs of the baby boom and are now forced to accept a greater proportion of a smaller high school graduating class simply to survive. As this is done, the signaling effects of a college degree become weaker than they were in the past. The mere possession of a college diploma is no guarantee that the innate and acquired talents of the degree recipient are equal to those of college graduates from previous generations. Therefore, those college students who are truly capable seek to distinguish themselves from the masses of college graduates who are benefiting from lower standards by graduating from institutions whose standards have been maintained. The result is that the more elite public and private institutions are receiving greater numbers of applicants than ever before, despite the fact that the total number of eighteen-year-olds is declining.

Although the overall decline in eighteen-year-olds is indisputable, the impact of such declines on various states and regions differs immensely. The so-called Rust Belt of the Northeast and Midwest has experienced and probably will continue to experience declines in population, including that of the traditional college-going age. In contrast, the South and West are experiencing growth due to the age composition of their populations, economic conditions, and migration. In discussing such regional differences, we face the problem that regions defined by the U.S. Bureau of the Census and the U.S. Department of Education are based on geography rather than on any economic or demographic reality. For example, the Northeast includes areas that are booming, such as Massachusetts, as well as states that are in serious decline because of the demise of certain heavy industries. The West includes border states that are heavily influenced by immigration from Mexico, along with states such as Wyoming or Montana that are remote from these effects.

Number of Traditional-Age Students Entering College

The most detailed breakdowns of populations by age come in the census years (years ending in zero). Thus, for 1980 we are able to learn the number of whites, blacks, and Hispanics of each age for the nation, regions, and states. We developed our initial projection of the number of eighteen-year-olds (the modal age of college entrants) by looking at individuals in each specific year of age from "under one" to eighteen. Ignoring the possibility that some individuals would die before they turn eighteen and, for the moment, the fact that there will be immigrants from other nations, we assumed that these age cohorts would translate directly into eighteen-year-olds in the future. That is, we assumed that all those who were seventeen-year-olds in 1980 would become eighteen-year-olds in 1981; those who were sixteen in 1980 would be the eighteen-year-olds in 1982; and so on until those currently under one year of age would turn eighteen in 1998. *(p. 36)*

National Trends. Based on the 1980 age distribution, there was a steady decline in the number of eighteen-year-olds between 1979 and 1986 for the nation as a whole. Beginning in

1986 there will have been a slight increase through 1989 and a subsequent decline from 1989 to 1992. Between 1979 and 1992 the total population of eighteen-year-olds in the United States will have fallen from 4,451,724 to 3,109,095. Between 1992 and 1997 the number of eighteen-year-olds will increase but only very moderately, from 3,109,095 to 3,269,557. The rate of growth will accelerate again after 1997, resulting in an eighteen-year-old population in 1998 of 3,533,692. During the nineteen years between 1979 and 1998, we will experience a decline of 21 percent in the number of eighteen-year-olds during the first seven years, an increase of 7 percent in the next three years, a decline of 17 percent in the next three years, and then an increase of 5 percent over the next five years, followed by an increase of 8 percent in the last year. At its low point in 1992, the number of eighteen-year-olds will be 30 percent below the number in 1979. At the end of the period, in 1998, the number of eighteen-year-olds will be 20 percent less than the number in 1979. Nationwide we would expect to see a drop of over 868,000 white eighteen-year-olds, a drop of 69,000 black eighteen-year-olds, and an increase of almost 34,000 Hispanic eighteen-year-olds by the year 1998.

Regional Variations. The changes in the composition and size of the eighteen-year-old cohort will vary substantially by region of the country. The decline in the number of eighteen-year-olds between 1979 and 1998 will be greatest in the Northeast, where the 1998 population of this group will be only 71 percent of the 1979 population. The next largest decline will be in the South, followed by the North Central region. The smallest decline in the number of eighteen-year-olds will be in the West, where the 1998 figure should be 89 percent of the 1979 figure. These patterns reflect only the age distribution of the population in each region in 1980 and do not take account of interregional migration and migration from abroad that might add to or detract from the population in a particular region.

If we look at population distribution by race from the 1980 census, there will be significant but not enormous changes in the percentage of eighteen-year-olds who are black or Hispanic in the four major census regions between 1980 and 1998 (Table 2.1). Each of the regions (Northeast, North Central, South, and West) will experience increases in the numbers of Hispanics and blacks, except for the West, where the percentage of blacks will actually fall.

Region-to-region migration has a relatively small impact on the college-age population of particular regions (Table 2.2). Whites account for the largest number of those who move from one region to another, although there is some movement of blacks as well. When comparing the net inflow or outflow of people aged five to twenty-four to the total number of eighteen-year-olds in a region, we find that the indigenous population is never affected by more than 12 percent in either direction. Because these extrapolations are based on 1985 data on five-to twenty-four-year-olds, they probably overestimate the change in the number of eighteen-year-olds in 1998.

Although the overall impact of internal migration may not be particularly significant in the broad regions we have considered, its impact on particular states will probably be greater. If most of the interregional migration to the West is concentrated in California, the impact there will clearly be greater than if this migration were distributed among all the states in that region.

The impact on certain states is even greater when we look at immigration from abroad. For each year between 1982 and 1986, between 79 and 86 percent of all foreign immigrants settled in only fifteen states—California, Connecticut, Florida, Missouri, Illinois, Maryland, Massachusetts, Michigan, New York, Mississippi, Ohio, Pennsylvania, Texas, Virginia, and Washington. Indeed, between 53 and 61 percent of all immigrants settled in just four states—California, Florida, New York, and Texas. Between 1982 and 1986 the concentration of immigrants in both the fifteen states and the four states increased (Immigration and Naturalization Service, 1988). It is reasonable to think that the distribution of eighteen-year-old immigrants mirrors the total immigrant distribution. Higher education institutions in states with large native minority populations will thus need to be cognizant of how immigrants from various areas of the world will distribute themselves among particular states.

Table 2.1 Population Distribution by Race and Region.

	White	Black	Hispanic	Total	% Black	% Hispanic	% Total Minorities
Northeast							
1979	783,562	100,998	54,910	939,470	10.8	5.8	16.6
1998	522,682	88,189	59,746	670,617	13.2	8.9	22.1
Northwest							
1979	1,028,453	116,661	30,512	1,175,626	9.9	2.6	12.5
1998	800,167	111,377	36,985	948,529	11.7	3.9	15.6
South							
1979	1,121,345	327,586	101,975	1,550,906	21.1	6.6	27.7
1998	849,836	287,694	102,626	1,240,156	23.2	8.3	31.5
West							
1979	654,631	54,763	146,705	856,099	6.4	17.1	23.5
1998	546,760	43,704	168,688	759,152	5.8	22.2	28.0

Source: U.S. Bureau of the Census (1980).

is capt.

Table 2.2. Region to Region Migration, 1984–85
All Movers, 1984–85. *(sources)*

6 column

	5–14 Years	15–24 Years	Net Migration	Total-18-Year-Olds 1998	Net Migration/Total 18-Year-Olds
Northeast					
Total	857,000	1,718,000	– 72,000	816,772	– 0.0882
White	653,000	1,456,000	– 84,000	664,234	– 0.1265
Black	185,000	233,000	11,000	99,193	0.1109
Midwest					
Total	1,669,000	2,759,000	– 47,000	963,447	– 0.0488
White	1,314,000	2,376,000	– 42,000	830,772	– 0.0506
Black	359,000	338,000	– 3,000	107,833	– 0.0278
South					
Total	2,476,000	4,018,000	64,000	1,263,848	0.0506
White	1,841,000	3,278,000	71,000	887,133	0.0800
Black	603,000	692,000	– 11,000	287,683	– 0.0382
West					
Total	1,597,000	2,549,000	56,000	672,489	0.0833
White	1,330,000	2,224,000	53,000	507,293	0.1045
Black	151,000	182,000	3,000	42,860	0.0700

R/T

Sources: U.S. Bureau of the Census, 1980, 1987a.

It is likely that the distribution by state of illegal immigrants, who add to the demand for higher education, closely parallels that of legal immigrants. We shall focus on the year 1986, and then refer to trends between 1982 and 1986 in immigration from Asia, Africa, Mexico, the Caribbean, and Central and South America. Immigrants from these areas, who are likely to be primarily members of minority groups, accounted for 87 percent of all immigrants in 1986, up from 86 percent in 1984.

In all but the case of Africa, over one-half of the immigrants from each of these regions settled in the four states of California, Florida, New York, and Texas. Of all immigrants from Asia, 80 percent went to the fifteen states that received the largest number of immigrants in 1982, and 86 percent went to those states in 1986 (Table 2.3). In certain states, particularly California, Florida, Illinois, New York, and Texas, a substantial

IS CAPT

Table 2.3 Immigration to Fifteen States. (source)

7 colin

Region	Total, 1982	Asia, 1982	Africa, 1982	Mexico, 1982	Caribbean, 1982	Central and S. Am., 1982
Total	594,131	313,291	14,314	56,106	67,379	59,074
% 15 States	0.7968	0.7841	0.7127	0.8314	0.8272	0.8498
Total 4 States	319,942	157,967	5,462	41,391	42,690	36,719
% 4 States	0.5385	0.5042	0.3816	0.7377	0.6336	0.6216
% California	0.2743	0.352	0.1736	0.3485	0.0192	0.1743
% Florida	0.0408	0.0135	0.0228	0.0101	0.1406	0.0945
% New York	0.1431	0.0749	0.1005	0.0081	0.4637	0.3225
% Texas	0.0802	0.0638	0.0847	0.3711	0.01	0.0302

7 colum,

Region	Total, 1986	Asia, 1986	Africa, 1986	Mexico, 1986	Caribbean, 1986	Central and S. Am., 1986
Total	601,708	268,248	17,463	66,533	101,632	70,254
% 15 States	0.8605	0.8441	0.7679	0.8621	0.9249	0.0929
Total 4 States	369,922	151,555	7,867	51,003	75,291	47,868
% 4 States	0.6148	0.565	0.4505	0.7666	0.7408	0.6814
% California	0.2805	0.3773	0.1732	0.4622	0.0353	0.206
% Florida	0.0808	0.0194	0.0301	0.0113	0.29	0.1116
% New York	0.1832	0.1152	0.1355	0.0099	0.4029	0.3253
% Texas	0.0703	0.053	0.1117	0.2833	0.0127	0.0384

R/T

Source: Immigration and Naturalization Service, 1988.

share of the total of the decline in eighteen-year-olds by the year 1998 due to declining birthrates will be compensated for by minority-group immigrants. In some states there will be dramatic increases in the proportion of the population that is minority by 1998. For example, in New York, our figures show that the eighteen-year-old minority population will increase from 26 percent to 44 percent between 1980 and 1998. In Florida, the proportion of minorities will rise from 29 percent to almost 41 percent. In Illinois, the minority share will go from almost 24 percent to over 32 percent. Comparable figures for Texas and California show increases from 38 percent to almost 49 percent and from 32 percent to almost 42 percent, respectively. Table 2.3

The minority shares in these states are underestimated because of the failure to account explicitly for the Asian population that was already in the United States in 1980. The Asian share will grow by the turn of the century not only as a result of immigration but also because of the age distribution of the existing Asian population in 1980. Moreover, if immigration from abroad continues at anywhere near the current rates until the end of the century, this factor will add dramatically to the share of minorities in those states that are the major recipients of immigrants. The increase in minorities stems from the decline in the number of domestic white eighteen-year-olds, the increase in certain native minority eighteen-year-olds, particularly Hispanics and Asians (but not blacks, who, along with whites, are projected to experience declines in numbers), and the increase in the number of immigrants who will be primarily minority.

Our universities and colleges will be forced to deal with a population that contains a larger number and share of minorities as well as substantially larger numbers of relatively new citizens. Whereas in earlier generations newcomers attempted to achieve assimilation in the "melting pot" of America, there is a much greater tendency for newly arrived immigrants to seek to maintain their cultural and linguistic identities. Thus, during their years of precollegiate education, they will probably have many more problems than was the case with earlier groups of immigrants and minorities. It is doubtful that in future years high school graduates will be entering college with the same set of acquired attitudes and aptitudes possessed by their predecessors.

Patterns of High School Completion

The next question to be addressed is, What proportion of those in the traditional secondary school–age cohort will actually graduate from high school in future years? We know that in October 1985, 68 percent of eighteen-year-olds and 82 percent of nineteen-year-olds had completed high school (U.S. Bureau of the Census, 1986). (Since the survey upon which these figures are based was taken in October, some eighteen-year-olds could still graduate in their eighteenth year.)

Prior to 1930, graduates as a percentage of the seventeen-year-old population did not exceed 30 percent, rising from roughly 2 percent in 1869–70 to 29 percent in 1929–30. By 1939–40, our nation had achieved a high school graduation rate (compared to the seventeen-year-old population) of over 50 percent, and the share of high school graduates had risen from 51 percent in 1939–40 to a peak of over 77 percent in 1968–69. The decade of the 1960s saw particularly high rates of high school graduation, usually over 75 percent. Since 1973, the proportion of seventeen-year-olds graduating from high school declined steadily until approximately 1980, when the figure was under 72 percent. Subsequently, the share of high school graduates has risen slightly, with the result that, in the last few years for which data are available, the rate is once again over 73 percent. Projections of college enrollments by the National Center for Education Statistics (referred to above) are based on the assumption that 73 percent of eighteen-year-olds will graduate from high school between 1983 and 1994 (U.S. Department of Education, Center for Education Statistics, 1987a, 1987b).

There are dramatic differences in high school completion rates according to race and Hispanic origin. For all eighteen- and nineteen-year-olds, the high school graduation rate was 73 percent in 1975 and 75 percent in 1985. The high school completion rates remained quite steady throughout this period. For whites, high school graduation rates for persons aged eighteen to nineteen were 76 percent in 1974 and 77 percent in 1985. In the early years of the 1980s, the white graduation rate fell to slightly under 75 percent. These figures contrast sharply with high school graduation rates for black eighteen- and nineteen-year-olds. These were only 56 percent in 1974 but rose rather steadily to 63 percent by 1985. The high school completion rate for Hispanics was 49 percent in 1974 and almost 50 percent in 1985.

When we look at high school graduation as a proportion of eighteen- to twenty-four-year-olds, the rates are substantially higher because the individuals involved have many more years in which to obtain their high school diplomas. The high school graduation rate for people eighteen to twenty-four years of age, for all races, was 81 percent in 1974 and 82 percent in 1984 (U.S. Bureau of the Census, 1986). For whites, the rate rose from 82.7 percent to 83 percent. Particularly encouraging is the fact that the 1974 black high school graduation rate for persons eighteen to twenty-four years old rose from 67 percent in 1974 to 75 percent in 1984. Similarly, the rate for those of Spanish origin rose from 56 percent to 60 percent. It is clear that members of nonwhite minorities are not precluded from achieving high school graduation even if they do not do so during their eighteenth or nineteenth years. Indeed, substantial numbers of these groups obtain their degrees after the age of nineteen.

The proportion of the selected age group that graduates from high school varies a great deal from state to state. At one end are states such as Florida and Mississippi, along with the District of Columbia, which have graduation rates of between 55 percent and 60 percent (of seventeen- and eighteen-year-olds). At the other extreme are states such as Minnesota, Nebraska, and Iowa, where graduation rates are approximately 85 percent. Part of the difference in high school graduation rates might be explained by the different racial mixes in different states. However, graduation rates might also be a function of the effectiveness of the public school systems and other socioeconomic circumstances in the various states. There is no clear category of superior and inferior states that is immediately apparent when we look at the data. However, it is most important to understand why certain states have high rates of high school completion and others do not.

We hypothesized that those states that were home to large numbers of a particular ethnic minority would tend to have relatively high rates of high school graduation for that minority. We reasoned that the political pressure to achieve high rates of high school graduation would increase with the size of the population concerned. In contrast, one might expect that minorities in states with very few of that minority group (for example, Hispanics in Maine) would do better than members of their race from largely minority areas, because they would be treated identically with their white peers. That is, the large number of blacks and Hispanics in cities such as New York and Los Angeles have led to de facto segregated high schools that are dominated by either blacks, Hispanics, or whites. To the extent that the quality of education provided in predominantly black and Hispanic high schools is inferior to that provided in high schools in more affluent white areas, the high school graduation rates of these students will be lower. Such segregation is not possible when there are only a few members of a minority group in a given area.

When we tested these competing hypotheses, we found that in states where there are more Hispanics, the percentage of Hispanics graduating from high school increases. Thus, our initial hypothesis was confirmed. But it is also true that a higher proportion of Hispanics is likely to graduate in states with a larger number of whites and in states with a smaller number of blacks. However, we could explain virtually nothing of the year-to-year or state-to-state differences in black high school graduation rates. Clearly, there are factors affecting black graduation rates that are not related to the size of cohorts.

Hispanics are more likely to graduate from high school in states where the overall graduation rate is high. When states undertake programs that lead to a reduction in dropout rates, Hispanics are clearly one of the groups benefiting. It appears that Hispanics are more successful when there are more whites and fewer blacks. Net of all the other factors in the model, living in a state further west resulted in an increase in high school graduation rates for Hispanics.

When we used the same variables to explain black high school graduation rates, only region was (negatively) correlated, indicating that blacks generally do better in the East and South than in the West. Where blacks constitute a large proportion of the population (the South), they are more likely to graduate from high school.

A study of historical trends makes it clear that the proportion of whites graduating from high school peaks at approximately 80 percent. It is also clear that high school graduation rates for both blacks and Hispanics are substantially below the 80 percent level but are rising at steady if slow rates. The problem of high school dropouts, particularly among minority groups, is at the top of most social priority lists at the present time. The dropout rate seems to be a measurable target at which politicians, corporate leaders, and others in our society can aim. There is thus every reason to be optimistic that minority rates of completion of high school will increase between now and the end of the century. It is also unlikely that rates of graduation of whites will increase very much, given their current high levels. These projections, along with the demographic trends discussed earlier, emphasize that the pool of students available to institutions of higher education will become increasingly dominated by minorities.

It should also be remembered that because of data limitations, nothing has been said about Asians, who have been exceptionally successful in American schools and colleges. They are less likely to drop out of high school than members of other minority groups and more likely to attend college once having graduated from high school. They have also accounted for the largest number of foreign immigrants in recent years. Thus, Asians will simply magnify the conclusions that we have drawn regarding the increasing dominance of minorities in American higher education.

The Current Population Reports enable us to analyze the progress (or lack thereof) that was made on the dropout problem by race for people between the ages of fourteen and thirty-four and eighteen and nineteen between 1975 and 1985 (U.S. Bureau of the Census, 1976b, 1986). Dropouts are defined as persons who are not enrolled in school and who are not high school graduates. Individuals who have received general equivalency diplomas are counted as graduates.

In 1975 and 1985, Hispanics were, by a wide margin, more likely to drop out of high school than were blacks or whites (Table 2.4). In most cases, women were more likely than men to improve their probability of obtaining a high school diploma over this ten-year period. In 1975, men were more likely to be dropouts than women, but this was reversed by 1985. For blacks, there was a more dramatic improvement: a 28.8 percent gain for men and a 37.7 percent gain for women. Hispanic men were more likely to drop out in 1985 than in 1975, whereas the dropout rate for Hispanic women improved.

IS CAPT·

Table 2.4. High School Dropouts,
by Race by Age Cohort, 14 to 34 Years Old and 18 to 19 Years Old. (sources)

| | 1975 | | 1985 | | % Change | % Change |
	14–34	18–19	14–34	18–19	14–34	18–19
White	12.8	14.7	11.5	13.8	0.8984	0.9388
Male	12.1	13.7	11.8	16.3	0.9752	1.1898
Female	13.5	15.6	11.1	11.3	0.8222	0.7244
Black	23.4	25.4	15.5	17.3	0.6624	0.6811
Male	21.9	27.7	15.6	17.7	0.7123	0.6390
Female	24.7	23.4	15.4	16.9	0.6235	0.7222
Hispanic	33.0	30.1	31.4	30.6	0.9515	1.0166
Male	29.0	26.3	32.1	42.2	1.0736	1.6046
Female	35.7	33.5	30.8	19.9	0.8627	0.5940

R/T

Sources: U.S. Bureau of the Census, 1976b, 1985c.

For the eighteen- and nineteen-year-old groups, whites and blacks showed higher dropout rates, indicating that some members of these groups may have obtained degrees later. Hispanics, in contrast, had lower dropout rates for eighteen- and nineteen-year-olds compared to the larger age span, probably indicating that Hispanics drop out earlier than members of other groups. The dropout rate for eighteen- and nineteen-year-old white and Hispanic males increased over this decade, while the rates improved for other racial and gender groups.

Rates of Progression into College

Once we know how many eighteen-year-olds of each race have graduated from high school, we can ask how many of these will enter college within the next year or so. In fact, these figures have remained relatively flat between 1974 and 1985 and are usually in the 40 to 50 percent range.

Approximately 45 percent of white high school graduates entered college when they were eighteen or nineteen in 1974. This percentage rose to around 49 percent over the next several years, and between 1979 and 1985 it rose from 48 percent to 56 percent. The share of black high school graduates aged eighteen to nineteen who entered college was 42 percent in 1974, rose for two years before falling to 46 percent in 1977, and then declined steadily between 1978 and 1985 to 39 percent. The Hispanic rate of progression from high school graduation to college entry in 1974 was higher than the ratio for either blacks or whites (49 percent) but since then has bounced around slightly, so that in 1985 the progression rate for Hispanics was 45 percent.

There is a substantially more diverse pattern of high school completion rates for whites, blacks, and Hispanics than there is for the progression rates of white, black, and Hispanic high school graduates into college. When these two ratios are combined, the percentage of population in college (which is the product of the high school graduation rate and the progression rate of high school graduates to college) is substantially higher for whites than for blacks and Hispanics. The share of eighteen- and nineteen-year-old blacks in college was above the share for Hispanics until 1983, after which time the two groups had approximately equal shares. The proportion of eighteen- and nineteen-year-old whites who were in college rose between 1974 and 1985 from 34 percent to 43 percent. The proportion for blacks was 23 percent in 1974, rose to 27 percent in 1981, but since then has fallen to 24 percent. For Hispanics, the 1974 share of the eighteen- and nineteen-year-old population in college was slightly under 24 percent. After reaching an all-time high of almost 27 percent in 1976, the share fell to 22 percent in 1985.

It appears that the primary bottleneck that prevents blacks and Hispanics from entering college when they are eighteen and nineteen years of age is their low rate of high school completion. Assuming that blacks and Hispanics are more likely to complete high school after the age of eighteen or nineteen, we should observe increased rates of college entry once members of these groups reach their twenties. Moreover, the data clearly reveal that anything that can be done to increase rates of high school graduation, short of lowering standards for blacks and Hispanics, will be beneficial. Not only do high school graduates have the opportunity to attend college but they are also more likely to be successful in the labor market and other aspects of life than those who drop out.

Since white progression rates have been rising in recent years, there is reason to hope that this same trend will be evidenced for other groups in the future, even though the progression rate of black high school graduates has fallen in recent years, whereas the Hispanic high school graduation rate has remained relatively steady.

    The most detailed data on participation in postsecondary education are available through the U.S. Department of Education's study *High School and Beyond,* which looked at the high school class of 1980 in the fall of 1980, 1981, 1982, and 1983 (U.S. Department of Education, Center for Education Statistics, 1984). Both socioeconomic status (SES) and ability are important determinants of the probability of moving from high school to college. Fully 68 percent of high school graduates in the highest SES quartile attended college on a full-time basis, but this share falls to 51 percent, 39 percent, and 29 percent as we move down to the lower quartiles. Similarly, 73 percent of those in the highest ability quartile attended college on a full-time basis the fall after high school graduation, but these shares decline to 58 percent, 37 percent, and 20 percent as we move down the ability quartiles. Persistence was greater among those in higher socioeconomic and ability groups. What we are not able to see is the cross-tabulation of socioeconomic status, ability, and race. That is, it is likely that minorities from low SES groups with high ability are somewhat constrained from attending college because of economic and related problems.

   Why These Differences? It is important to identify the reasons for these divergent patterns of progression of high school graduates to college. Economic patterns clearly play a role. The desperate poverty facing many black and Hispanic communities clearly put pressure on youngsters from those groups to drop out of high school or, even if they have completed high school, to look for a job rather than attend college. In recent years, rising college costs and a decline in the availability of many types of need-based financial aid have deterred many minorities from attending college.

   Arguments that the truly needy still have access to funds to pay for college fly in the face of evidence of the declining share of black high school graduates who are enrolling in college. Part of the problem here is that even if black and Hispanic graduates have access to funds that can cover all the tuition costs and even perhaps the incidental expenses that go along with college attendance, funds are rarely available to cover the earnings forgone by such youngsters when they enter college instead of taking even the most menial types of jobs. Many minority high school graduates cannot afford the luxury of deferring income when they see younger siblings and parents living in abject poverty. Thus, even if they are qualified for college admittance, and even if they can obtain funds to pay for their college expenses, their need to support their families takes precedence over their desire to enter college. Rising teenage pregnancy rates in the minority communities are another reason why college is out of the question for many minorities (Wilson, 1987).

Nevertheless, if policymakers would only recognize the economic pressures on minority students, it would at least theoretically be possible to begin reducing such pressures. Despite the severe deficits in the federal budget and some state budgets, perhaps the most effective expenditures of public funds and private philanthropy are those directed toward providing the support that would enable minorities to enter college and thereby begin working to break the cycle of poverty.

It is not sufficient to develop policies that ensure that any qualified member of a minority group will have his or her out-of-pocket college costs covered. Until the opportunity costs of attending college rather than joining the labor force are taken into consideration, the decision to enter college will always be a difficult one for many low SES and minority youth. The need to work whether or not one attends college is probably the primary factor explaining the patterns of enrollment of minorities by institutional type to be discussed below. The community colleges in many states are unique in that they take into account the need for their students to work full time. Thus, they are the only choice for students who must earn more than is currently available from scholarship programs.

A second set of factors explaining the lower rates of progression from high school graduation to college attendance for minorities compared to whites involves the nature of the education obtained during the high school years. From 1974 to 1979, there was little discernible difference among progression rates for whites, blacks, and Hispanics. Since 1979, the progression rates for whites have risen slowly while those for blacks and Hispanics have fallen. By 1985, 56 percent of white high school graduates went on to college, 45 percent of Hispanic graduates went on to college, but only 38 percent of black high school graduates did so.

These gaps have widened precisely during a period when pressure to reduce high school dropout rates and to increase high school graduation rates has mounted. One way of increasing the probability of high school graduation is to reduce standards. But if, in order to increase minority graduation rates from high school, more minorities are tracked into general and vocational programs rather than into college preparatory programs, it is logical to expect a smaller proportion of minority graduates to enter college.

Moreover, if standards are lowered to such an extent that work that previously would have led to failing grades and dismissal from high school is now viewed as acceptable to meet graduation standards, then it is also understandable why those who receive a high school diploma either do not go on to college or, once enrolled, fail to receive a degree. There have been a number of efforts in recent years to ensure that the high school diploma does not become a devalued degree. Nevertheless, it is ironic that at a time when high school completion rates for blacks and Hispanics are rising, progression rates from high school graduation to college are falling for these same groups. It is necessary to get beyond the notion of a "quick fix" to the problem of low rates of high school graduation for minorities. If the political and financial pressure on public high schools to lessen their dropout rates were to be converted into attempts to provide minorities with real preparation for subsequent college study, it is possible that minority progression rates to college would increase over the next decade or so.

Several questions arise with regard to such a policy. First, will educational leaders at the high school level ever be able to take a long view and insist upon appropriate graduation requirements even if that means higher dropout rates and lower

graduation rates for minorities in the short run? Second, even
if this longer view were accepted, are the socioeconomic circumstances of many impoverished minorities such that higher
standards will actually result in more graduates with a real
preparation for college? Are we facing a crisis that is purely
educational, or are we facing more deeply ingrained social problems such as teenage pregnancy, gangs, drugs, the disintegra-
tion of the family, and the like? Clearly, some schools are
underfunded, and the quality and motivation of our teaching
force may be lower than they were in previous generations. But
can any level of funding and any level of teacher ability and
training ever compensate for the dismal circumstances facing
many minority youth today? If these social problems can be successfully attacked, there is no question that the representation
of minorities in our institutions of higher education will increase.

   College Choice. Between 1970 and 1981, the fifty states
and the District of Columbia together experienced a 26 percent
increase in first-time enrollments in their institutions of higher
education (American Council on Education, 1987). Between
1981 and 1984 this trend was reversed, as first-time enrollments
declined by 9 percent. Twice as many states experienced declines
in their first-time enrollments in all institutions as experienced
increases. The range was from a 23 percent decline in Nebraska,
a 20 percent decline in New Jersey, a 20 percent decline in South
Dakota, a 16 percent decline in South Carolina, and a 16 percent decline in Colorado, to a 22 percent increase in California, a 30 percent increase in Illinois, and an 84 percent increase
in Nevada. In general, except for the Rocky Mountain and Far
West regions, the decline in the independent sector was greater
than in the public sector. Since total enrollment declined by only
1 percent between 1981 and 1984, it is clear that the decline
in first-time enrollment was more than compensated for by returning students and by students who took longer to complete
their education than in the past. But stability in the number
of first-time enrollments nationally does not necessarily mean
that particular states or regions are experiencing this same
stability.

The Center for Education Statistics has calculated the percent of minorities by states enrolled in institutions of higher education in the fall of 1984 (U.S. Department of Education, 1987a, 1987b). The percent of minority students is based on the total enrollment of U.S. citizens (total enrollment less enrollment of nonresident aliens). Overall, 17 percent of those enrolled in institutions of higher education in the United States in the fall of 1984 were minorities. The range was from 71 percent in Hawaii, 40 percent in the District of Columbia, 34 percent in New Mexico, 30 percent in Mississippi, 30 percent in California, 27 percent in Louisiana, and 25 percent in Texas to lows of 5 percent in Idaho, 4 percent in Minnesota, Wyoming, and Iowa, 3 percent in New Hampshire, 2 percent in Vermont, and 1 percent in Maine.

These wide variations in the minority representation in higher education result in part from the differential distribution of minorities across states. Related to this is the extent to which various racial/ethnic groups are represented in colleges in the same proportion as they are represented in the overall college-age population. That is, racial groups do not enroll at rates equivalent to their population in a state. To illustrate this point we will refer to the states of California and Texas (Kaufman, cited in Gosman, 1986). In California, although the college-age population was 72 percent white, only 68 percent of the undergraduates enrolled in 1984–85 were white. Similarly, in Texas, 76 percent of the college-age population was white, whereas 72 percent of undergraduate enrollments in 1984–85 were white. In California, 9 percent of the college-age population was black, whereas 7 percent of the enrollments in 1984–85 were black; the comparable figures for Texas were 13 percent and 9 percent.

While both whites and blacks were somewhat underrepresented in undergraduate enrollments in these two states, the underrepresentation of Hispanics was much more pronounced. In California, although 23 percent of the college-age population was Hispanic in 1984–85, only 10 percent of enrollments were Hispanic; in Texas the comparable figures were 22 percent and 13 percent. In both California and Texas, American

Indian enrollments were at least equal to the proportion of American Indians in the college-age population. In California, 1 percent of the population and 1 percent of enrollments were American Indian, and in Texas 0.3 percent of both the population and enrollments were American Indian. The situation for Asians was quite the opposite of what we have seen for the other groups. In California, although 5 percent of the college-age population was Asian, 10 percent of enrollments in 1984–85 were Asian; and in Texas 2 percent of enrollments were Asian although only 0.8 percent of the population were members of that ethnic group.

Different states may also have quite different shares of minorities in their colleges and universities because of the fact that students, particularly white students, often leave their state of residence to attend college. Since blacks and Hispanics in particular are more likely to be members of low SES groups, they are also more likely to remain at home to attend college (U.S. Department of Education, 1987b; American Council on Education, 1987). Fourteen states have net outmigration of students attending college. These range from New Jersey, which lost 36,000 students net in 1984, to the state of Washington, which lost a net of 85 students. For the United States as a whole the ratio of students remaining in their state of residence to all students who are residents of that state was 86 percent. Among those states retaining the largest share of their resident students were Arizona, California, Louisiana, Michigan, Mississippi, North Carolina, Texas, and Wisconsin. Those retaining the fewest of their resident students were Alaska, the District of Columbia, New Hampshire, and New Jersey. To the extent that more whites than minorities leave a state, the share of minorities in institutions of higher education in that state will of course rise.

Institutions in a particular state can thus combat declining undergraduate enrollments by trying to retain as many of their own residents as possible. In addition, institutions can attempt to attract students from other states. This is a particularly useful policy for private institutions. However, public institutions are under pressure to satisfy the enrollment demands from within their own state before they begin looking elsewhere, and out-of-state students may be viewed as receiving an unwarranted subsidy.

Perhaps the most important question regarding college choice is how first-time full-time freshmen sort themselves into various types of institutions. The share of each racial group attending highly selective private institutions, the most elite group of institutions, is very small (overall, it is approximately 1.2 percent of all students). Between 1976 and 1984, Asians were the racial group most likely to attend these institutions, as their share rose from 1.4 percent to 2.5 percent over the period. Alien residents' share in highly selective private institutions rose from 1.6 percent to 2.2 percent. The white share was 1.2 percent in 1976, and this rose to 1.5 percent in 1984. Hispanics, blacks, and American Indians generally saw less than 0.5 percent of their first-time full-time freshmen attending highly selective private institutions.

In general, all races, but particularly Hispanics, are most likely to begin their college careers in public two-year colleges. It is well known that individuals who begin in two-year colleges have a low probability of continuing to completion of the bachelor's degree; the transfer rate is generally under 10 percent. Thus, one way for four-year institutions to increase their enrollments during a period of overall declining enrollments is to encourage two-year college students to transfer after they receive their A.A. degrees. The problem is that a high proportion of two-year college students drop out even before completing the A.A. degree. High priority must be given to ensuring the persistence of two-year college students and their subsequent transfer to four-year institutions.

Of course, one of the underlying questions here is whether or not students enrolling in two-year colleges, particularly those who select vocational programs, really want more than an A.A. degree and, indeed, whether they would really do better in the labor market if they achieved a higher degree. Although some people in the four-year sector consider any students who do not achieve a bachelor's degree to be failures, this certainly is not always the case. Going to college for one or two years may well represent a greater achievement than not going at all, and the fact is that the bachelor's degree need not be the objective of every high school graduate.

Overall, private universities attract small proportions of minority groups except Asians. There are many reasons for this pattern, including the higher tuition costs and, often, the higher admission standards at these schools. As long as there were substantial numbers of middle-class whites, private institutions could afford to be less than active in recruiting minorities. However, because the number of whites will decline between now and the end of the century, private institutions will find it necessary to reconsider their recruitment patterns and to strive to obtain more financial aid to support minority applicants.

There will be a great deal of interinstitutional competition for students over the next decade, and much of this competition will be for minority students. However, for a given pool of minority students, such competition is a zero-sum game. It would be much more fruitful to work at enlarging the pool. There will also be continued competition from the military and from the job market. Both of these are becoming increasingly attractive options, particularly for low SES high school graduates because they are likely to receive job-related training and are not required to forgo a full-time income.

Conclusion

This chapter has attempted to outline the demographic changes that will face institutions of higher education by the turn of the century. Based on the age distribution of the current population in the United States and some reasonable assumptions about immigration from abroad, it is clear that the eighteen-year-old population available to consider higher education by the year 2000 will be much more ethnically diverse than has been the case in the past. In particular, the share of Hispanics and Asians in the eighteen-year-old cohort will rise dramatically over the next fifteen years.

The increase of Hispanics in college in recent years is due to an overall increase in the Hispanic population and is not the result of a rise in the college-going rate of Hispanic young adults

(Freund, 1988). This is probably also the explanation for the growth in the number of Asian students. Hispanics and blacks have unquestionably been educationally disadvantaged throughout the recent history of this nation. Although Asians have been the most successful ethnic group in regard to education, a significant probability exists that recent immigrants from certain parts of the Asian world will more closely resemble other minorities than has been the case for Asians in the past. These changing circumstances lead us to anticipate that the job of providing higher education to our nation's youth will become an increasingly difficult one. By extrapolating the current characteristics of minorities, we conclude that the typical eighteen-year-old college entrant will be less well prepared for college than were his or her recent predecessors.

The real question is the extent to which we are justified in extrapolating from the past in making predictions about the nature of minorities by the turn of the century. Clearly, one of the recent movements to improve secondary education has been motivated by the decline in student achievement in that segment. To the extent that this decline has been the result of the changing ethnic composition of the high school class, it might be that improvements aimed at dealing with the new demographics will result in a minority cohort that is better prepared for college. An optimistic view would be that by the year 2000, when minorities constitute a greater share of those considering college, we will find minorities who are better prepared for college and more closely resemble their white peers than has been the case to date. But if a larger share of eighteen-year-olds retains the characteristics of minorities as they are today, substantial adjustments will be required by the higher education system.

Such adjustments will include the necessity to change recruiting policies (perhaps including standards for admission) and to increase the availability of financial aid. Commenting on a recent report by the U.S. Department of Education that the level of black enrollments has remained essentially stable over the last decade after a period of great growth from the mid 1960s to the mid 1970s, Patricia Smith, the director of legislative analysis for the American Council on Education, said, "The concern is not so much that the number is down (26,000 below the peak of 1,107,000 in 1980), but that we're not making great progress toward increasing it" ("Minorities' Share of College Enrollments Edges Up," 1988).

It is likely that a larger proportion of resources will have to be spent on remediation, that is, underprepared students will have to be brought up to the level where they can deal with college courses. Greater efforts will have to be made to advise and counsel students if they are to actually complete the programs in which they enroll. And greater concern with the transfer function of two-year colleges will have to be demonstrated.

The next twenty years can be seen as a time of crisis in higher education, or they can be seen as a period of opportunity. It is tempting to place the responsibility on institutions other than those in the postsecondary system, such as the family, social service agencies, and particularly the secondary schools. However, it is likely that whatever improvements are made in these areas, the responsibility for the postsecondary education of our nation's youth will remain with the colleges and universities in this country. As the nature of the student body continues to change, this will remain a major challenge.

[1]When we compared our projections of eighteen-year-olds, which were based directly upon the number of individuals of each year of age from the 1980 census, to a projection made by the U.S. Bureau of the Census, we found that our simple approach yielded almost identical results to the figures in the Current Population Reports (CPR) (U.S. Bureau of the Census, 1983a). In 1982, our figures matched almost exactly; but, because of immigration acounted for in the CPR report, ours became progressively smaller compared to the CPR estimate. However, by 1995 our projection is still 96 percent of the CPR estimate.

References

American Council on Education. *Fact Book on Higher Education.* London: Collier MacMillian, 1987.

Dresch, S. P. "Democracy, Technology, and Higher Education: Toward a Formal Model of Educational Adaptation." *Journal of Political Economy,* 1975, *83* (3), 535–569.

Freeman, R. B. *The Overeducated American.* New York: Academic Press, 1976.

Freund, W. H. *Trends in Minority Enrollment in Higher Education 1976–1986.* Washington, D.C.: U.S. Government Printing Office, 1988.

Gosman, E. "Population Characteristics and College Attendance." Unpublished manuscript, 1986.

Immigration and Naturalization Service. "Immigrants Admitted by Country of Birth." Unpublished raw data, 1988.

"Minorities Share of College Enrollments Edges Up." *Chronicle of Higher Education,* Mar. 9, 1988, pp. A33, 35, 36.

"Mostly Stable: College and University Enrollments 1985–1991." *Chronicle of Higher Education,* Nov. 25, 1987, p. A29.

O'Neill, D., and Sepielli, P. *Education in the United States: 1940–83.* Washington, D.C.: U.S. Government Printing Office, 1985.

Solmon, L. C., and Banks, D. "The Future of Higher Education in the United States." Paper prepared for the Ford Foundation Symposium on Demographics, New York, Apr. 1988.

Solmon, L. C., and Ochsner, N. L. *College Education and Employment — The Recent Graduates.* Bethlehem, Pa.: CPC Foundation, 1979.

U.S. Bureau of the Census. *School Enrollment — Social and Economic Characteristics of Students: October 1974.* Current Population Reports, Series P-20, no. 286. Washington, D.C.: U.S. Government Printing Office, 1975.

U.S. Bureau of the Census. *Household and Family Characteristics: March 1976.* Current Population Reports, Series P-20, no. 311. Washington, D.C.: U.S. Government Printing Office, 1976a.

U.S. Bureau of the Census. *School Enrollment — Social and Economic Characteristics of Students: October 1975.* Current Population Reports, Series P-20, no. 303. Washington, D.C.: U.S. Government Printing Office, 1976b.

U.S. Bureau of the Census. *School Enrollment — Social and Economic Characteristics of Students: October 1976.* Current Population Reports, Series P-20, no. 319. Washington, D.C.: U.S. Government Printing Office, 1978.

U.S. Bureau of the Census. *School Enrollment — Social and Economic Characteristics of Students: October 1977.* Current Population Reports, Series P-20, no. 333. Washington, D.C.: U.S. Government Printing Office, 1979a.

U.S. Bureau of the Census. *School Enrollment — Social and Economic Characteristics of Students: October 1978.* Current Population Reports, Series P-20, no. 346. Washington, D.C.: U.S. Government Printing Office, 1979b.

U.S. Bureau of the Census. *U.S. Summary Tables.* Washington, D.C.: U.S. Government Printing Office, 1980.

U.S. Bureau of the Census. *School Enrollment — Social and Economic Characteristics of Students: October 1979.* Current Population Reports, Series P-20, no. 360. Washington, D.C.: U.S. Government Printing Office, 1981a.

U.S. Bureau of the Census. *School Enrollment — Social and Economic Characteristics of Students: October 1980.* Current Population Reports, Series P-20, no. 362. Washington, D.C.: U.S. Government Printing Office, 1981b.

U.S. Bureau of the Census. *Provisional Projections of the Population of States by Age and Sex: 1980–2000.* Current Population Reports, Series P-25, no. 937. Washington, D.C.: U.S. Government Printing Office, 1983a.

U.S. Bureau of the Census. *School Enrollment — Social and Economic Characteristics of Students: October 1981.* Current Population Reports, Series P-20, no. 373. Washington, D.C.: U.S. Government Printing Office, 1983b.

U.S. Bureau of the Census. *Education Attainment in the United States: March 1981 and 1980.* Current Population Reports, Series P-20, no. 390. Washington, D.C.: U.S. Government Printing Office, 1984.

U.S. Bureau of the Census. *Geographic Mobility: 1985.* Current Population Reports, Series P-20, no. 420. Washington, D.C.: U.S. Government Printing Office, 1985a.

U.S. Bureau of the Census. *School Enrollment — Social and Economic Characteristics of Students: October 1981 and 1980.* Current Population Reports, Series P-20, no. 400. Washington, D.C.: U.S. Government Printing Office, 1985b.

U.S. Bureau of the Census. *School Enrollment — Social and Economic Characteristics of Students: October 1984.* Current Population Reports, Series P-20, no. 404. Washington, D.C.: U.S. Government Printing Office, 1985c.

U.S. Bureau of the Census. *School Enrollment — Social and Economic Characteristics of Students: October 1985.* Current Population

Reports, Series P-20, no. 409. Washington, D.C.: U.S. Government Printing Office, 1986.

U.S. Bureau of the Census. *Geographic Mobility: 1985.* Current Population Reports, Series P-20, no. 420. Washington, D.C.: U.S. Government Printing Office, 1987a.

U.S. Bureau of the Census. *School Enrollment — Social and Economic Characteristics of Students: October 1983.* Current Population Reports, Series P-20, no. 413. Washington, D.C.: U.S. Government Printing Office, 1987b.

U.S. Department of Education, Center for Education Statistics. *Conditions of Education.* Washington, D.C.: U.S. Government Printing Office, 1983.

U.S. Department of Education, Center for Education Statistics. *High School and Beyond.* Washington, D.C.: U.S. Government Printing Office, 1984.

U.S. Department of Education, Center for Education Statistics. *Condition of Education.* Washington, D.C.: U.S. Government Printing Office, 1985.

U.S. Department of Education, Center for Education Statistics. *Digest of Educational Statistics.* Washington, D.C.: U.S. Government Printing Office, 1986.

U.S. Department of Education, Center for Education Statistics *Condition of Education.* Washington, D.C.: U.S. Government Printing Office, 1987a.

U.S. Department of Education, Center for Education Statistics. *Digest of Educational Statistics.* Washington, D.C.: U.S. Government Printing Office, 1987b.

U.S. Department of Education, Center for Education Statistics. *Projections of Educational Statistics to 1992–93.* Washington, D.C.: U.S. Government Printing Office, 1987c.

"U.S. Department of Education HEGIS Data Reported." *Chronicle of Higher Education,* July 23, 1986.

Wilson, W. J. *The Truly Disadvantaged.* Chicago: University of Chicago Press, 1987.

E/o Chap. 2

🍂 3

Hispanics

(sf)

by *Gary Orfield*

If existing trends continue, there are going to be a great many more young Hispanics in our schools and colleges in the coming decades than there are now, and these students are going to have very serious educational problems. Hispanic enrollment has more than doubled in this generation, but the schools are not serving as an avenue into the mainstream for most Hispanics. If the current pattern of relationships between education, jobs, and income holds, and the current projections about the kinds of jobs to be created in the economy are fulfilled, inadequate education for what will become the nation's largest minority group will have profound and lasting social and economic consequences.

This chapter presents data through the 1986–87 academic year to show the enormous growth of Hispanic enrollment in U.S. schools and colleges since the 1960s, to describe the intensifying segregation of Hispanic students and the inequality of the schools in which they are segregated, and to discuss dropout rates and the pattern of declining college access among Hispanics.[1] Except in Florida, Hispanics are moving backwards in the field of higher education in every state where they are present in large numbers.

NOTE
(p. 58)

Growth of Hispanic Enrollment

Since 1968, when the federal government first began to collect data on school enrollments, there has been enormous

40

growth in the proportion of Hispanic public school students and a substantial decline in the proportion of Anglos, or non-Hispanic whites (see Table 3.1). Hispanic students made up 4.6 percent of the national total in the fall of the 1968–69 school year but accounted for 9.9 percent in the 1986–87 school year. In this eighteen-year period, in other words, the Hispanic share of the total U.S. public school enrollment more than doubled. *Table 3.1*

Table 3.1. Percentage National Enrollment by Race and Ethnicity, Fall 1968 to Fall 1986. *(Sources)*

	1968	1980	1986	Change
Hispanic* NOTE"	4.6	8.0	9.9	+ 5.3
Black	14.5	16.1	16.1	+ 1.6
Anglo* NOTE"	80.0	73.2	70.4	− 9.6
Asian and Indian	0.9	2.7	3.7	+ 2.8

*Hispanics may be of any race; Anglos are non-Hispanic whites.

Sources: DBS Corporation, 1982, 1987.

Eighteen years ago there were more than three times as many blacks as Hispanics in the school population; now, Hispanic enrollment is nearly two-thirds that of black enrollment. There was one Hispanic student for every seventeen white students eighteen years ago; in 1986–87 there was one for every seven whites. Should these trends continue, they will fundamentally change the social structure of American education. Hispanics will become the nation's largest minority group and the proportion of whites will fall substantially. All signs show that these changes are continuing. Census reports show that the Hispanic population has been growing five times as fast as the overall population in the 1980s.

Between 1968 and 1986 the number of Hispanic students in public schools grew from 2,003,000 to 4,064,000, an increase of 2.1 million students, while white enrollment dropped 5.7 million and black enrollment increased only a modest 0.3 million. During this period, in other words, Hispanic enrollment increased by 103 percent, Anglo enrollment dropped 16 percent, and black enrollment was up 5 percent. Asian and American Indian enrollments increased even more dramatically than did Hispanic enrollment but began at a much lower baseline. Asian enrollment increased an astonishing 55 percent in the six years from 1980 to 1986 (Table 3.2).

Table 3.2. Enrollment Changes, 1968–1986 (in Millions).

	1968	1980	1986	Change
Hispanics	2.00	3.18	4.06	+ 2.06
Anglos	34.70	29.16	28.96	− 5.74
Blacks	6.28	6.42	6.62	+ .34

Sources: DBS Corporation, 1982, 1987.

There is no sign that these trends will fundamentally change. During the most recent two years for which data are available (from fall 1984 to fall 1986), the pattern was generally similar, except for a small upturn for Anglo students from their 1984 low point. This upturn reflects the temporary surge in the Anglo birthrate that occurred during the late 1970s and early 1980s, but this birthrate is likely to decline once the baby-boom generation moves out of the childbearing years. Meanwhile, black enrollment increased 0.2 million, Hispanic, 0.5 million, and Asian, 0.2 million. These trends clearly show that the proportion of whites in the schools will continue to decline as the minority population becomes increasingly diverse and much more heavily Hispanic.

The nation's Hispanic population and enrollment have long been concentrated in the states of the Southwest and the metropolitan regions of New York, Chicago, and Miami. Eight states enroll a total of 3.57 million Hispanic students, 88 percent of the national total. Census estimates (Table 3.3) show that these states contain about 40 percent of the nation's total population ("Florida Supplants Pennsylvania . . . ," 1987). The great majority of the increase in Hispanic enrollments took place in California and Texas, which have long educated most American Hispanics. These two states had three of every five Hispanic students in the 1986–87 academic year.

California is by far the nation's most populous state, and census projections suggest that Texas will replace New York as _is capt_

Table 3.3. States with Largest Hispanic Enrollments, 1970–1986. _(sources)_

	1986 Enrollment	1970 Enrollment	Change Number	%
California	1,381,100	706,900	674,200	95
Texas	1,086,200	565,700	520,500	92
New York	384,700	316,600	68,100	21
Illinois	157,000	78,100	78,900	101
Arizona	154,700	85,500	69,200	81
Florida	149,500	65,700	83,800	127
New Jersey	132,000	59,100	72,900	123
New Mexico	128,900	109,300	19,600	18

R/T

Sources: DBS Corporation, 1982, 1987.

the second most populous by 1995 ("Population Mark Is Seen for Texas . . . ," 1988). Hispanic enrollment in both of these important states almost doubled between 1968 and 1986.

Among the states with large Hispanic populations, the increase was least rapid in New Mexico and New York. New Mexico is the state with the largest proportion of Hispanic students (45 percent in 1986). New Mexico has had less than 2 percent growth in overall public school enrollment in the sixteen-year period from 1970 to 1986 and is not a major destination for contemporary Hispanic migration. The state has many Spanish-American or Hispano families who have resided there for generations. New York has a smaller total statewide enrollment than it had in 1970, and the proportion of Hispanic students is up only modestly from 9 percent to 12 percent. Migration from Puerto Rico, which accounts for a very substantial share of the state's Hispanic students, has long passed its peak.

Aside from California and Texas, which have very large and youthful Hispanic populations and continuous mass migration across their borders, there are several different kinds of states and metropolitan areas that have experienced rapid Hispanic growth. The Chicago and Miami areas are large centers of Hispanic migration, which attract Hispanics from a variety of locations, although most of the Hispanics in Chicago are of Mexican origin and Miami is the great center of Cuban settlement. Both cities have a well-developed infrastructure of Hispanic institutions and labor markets. Hispanics have acquired a great deal of financial and political power in Miami.

The other large growth areas, Arizona and New Jersey, are showing the effects of extremely rapid economic growth and urbanization in areas near large Hispanic settlements. Both the Valley of the Sun region around Phoenix and the northern New Jersey suburbs have been major economic boom areas since the 1960s. Hispanic migration is strongly influenced by both economic opportunity and the presence of a Hispanic community.

The future may bring similar patterns of increasing Hispanic enrollments in new centers of economic growth, particularly if they are near existing Hispanic settlement areas and already have significant local Hispanic communities. Young families seeking economic opportunity are highly mobile, and a great many Hispanic families are young and looking for jobs.

Recent patterns in population changes show where the greatest growth is now concentrated. With the exception of New Mexico, all the states with the largest Hispanic enrollments had substantial increases in those enrollments during the first six years of the 1980s. The smallest increase, 18 percent, was in New York state, while all the other states had from 26 percent to 38 percent increases. In the most recent two-year period, the largest increase in the number of Hispanic students was in Texas, where a recent Supreme Court decision, *Pyler* v. *Doe*, 457 U.S. 202 (1982), required the public schools to enroll children of un-documented families, reversing the state's previous policy. The other largest proportionate increases came in Arizona, New Jersey, and Illinois.

These trends suggest that the existing centers of Hispanic settlement are likely to see a steadily increasing presence of Hispanic students in all their educational institutions. Several of these states are among the most rapidly growing in overall population and political power. The growth of Hispanic enrollment is not yet fully apparent in secondary and postsecondary education because the Hispanic population is very young, it continues to drop out of high school at a high rate, and the fraction of Hispanic graduates going on to college has declined since the 1970s. In 1985, only 59 percent of Hispanics aged twenty to twenty-four had finished high school (U.S. Bureau of the Census, 1987a). The 1987 data show 60 percent of Hispanics had graduated from high school, compared to 77 percent of blacks and 86 percent of whites (U.S. Bureau of the Census, 1987a). During the 1980s, the proportion of Hispanic high school graduates enrolling in college has dropped.

The Hispanic proportion of high school graduates is far below their proportion of total enrollment in secondary education. In 1986, 9.9 percent of the nation's students were Hispanic, but only 5.9 percent of the new graduates and 5 percent of all college students were Hispanics. In New Mexico, which has a stable Hispanic population and a large number of Hispanics whose families have been in the United States for generations, the ratio was much closer: 45 percent of the students and 42 percent of the high school graduates were Hispanics. New York's record was one of the worst: Hispanics made up 12 percent of the total enrollment but only 5 percent of the graduates. Illinois's record was similar: Hispanics accounted for 9 percent of the state's students but only 4 percent of its 1986–87 high school graduates. Florida, like Illinois, has a 9 percent Hispanic statewide enrollment but twice as high a proportion of its 1986 graduates (8 percent) were Hispanic.

Although many different factors contribute to these statistics, the striking national gap between the number of Hispanics who are enrolled in schools and the number who graduate, along with the extraordinary variation among states, is an indication of both a general problem and different regional outcomes that deserve careful investigation (DBS Corporation, 1987). Hispanics have very serious educational problems in most areas where they are concentrated in large numbers, although this is not true for the Florida area, where the nation's Cuban Americans are concentrated.

State higher education officials must compare their enrollments with the percent of their state's high school graduates who are Hispanic. A university system should not point with pride to a 10 percent increase in Hispanic enrollment, for example, if the state's pool of college-eligible Hispanic students went up 25 percent during the same period.

New Mexico leads the list in 1986–87 with 42 percent Hispanics among new high school graduates, followed by Texas with 25 percent, Arizona 19 percent, California 18 percent, Colorado 9 percent, Florida 8 percent, New Jersey 6 percent, and New York, Nevada, and Wyoming all 5 percent. The future of higher education in several states depends to a significant degree on encouraging enrollment and graduation among Hispanics, whose numbers are very likely to continue to increase. If we compare 1986 high school graduate data with college enrollment data for the same year, it is apparent that a disproportionate share of Hispanics do not make the transition to college (Table 3.4). Forty-two percent of New Mexico's high school

IS CAPT·

~~Table 3.4.~~ Percentage of Hispanic Students, High School Graduates, and College Students, 1986–87, in Selected States. (sources)

	Total Public School Enrollment	High School Graduates	Total College Students
Arizona	26	19	9
California	27	18	11
Florida	9	8	10
Illinois	9	4	5
New Jersey	11	6	6
New Mexico	45	42	26
New York	12	5	7
Texas	33	25	15

R/T

Sources: DBS Corporation, 1987; "Table of Civil Rights Statistics," 1988.

graduates were Hispanics, but this figure falls to 26 percent for its college students. In Texas, 25 percent of the high school diplomas went to Hispanics, but Hispanics accounted for only 15 percent of college enrollment. Arizona reported that 19 percent of its high school graduates were Hispanic but that its colleges had less than half as large a proportion of Hispanics (9 percent). California had 18 percent Hispanics coming out of its secondary schools but only 11 percent in the colleges. Florida, in striking contrast, not only graduates a much higher proportion of its Hispanics from high school, but the proportion of Hispanics in college is actually higher than the proportion in the pool of high school graduates (10 percent compared to 8 percent). Table 3.4

Table 3.4

Precollegiate Problems and College Preparation. Hispanic students are in less competitive high schools than white or Asian students, and they confront special problems in getting ready for college. They very often find themselves in highly segregated settings that are becoming even more segregated over time. This situation stands in contrast to that of black students, who have become much less segregated, particularly in the South, and who have reached a level of integration that has remained virtually unchanged into the mid 1980s. Asian students, in striking contrast to Hispanics, typically attend schools with large white majorities. In terms of college preparation, the important factor is that the segregated Hispanic schools tend to be schools with high proportions of low-income students, low proportions of middle-class students, high dropout rates, low achievement scores, and, in general, much less adequate preparation for college (Table 3.5). This isolation from the educational mainstream

Table 3.5. Hispanic Segregation by Region, 1968–1984. *(source)*

| | % of Students in Predominantly White Schools | | % of Students in 90 to 100% Minority Schools | |
	1968	*1984*	*1968*	*1984*
West	58	46	12	23
South	30	32	34	37
Northeast	25	25	44	47
Midwest	68	22	7	24
U.S.	45	29	23	31

Source: Office for Civil Rights Data Tapes, unpublished; Orfield and Montfort, 1988.

in high school means that few Hispanic students come to college from schools that have the level of curriculum and expectations that typical white and Asian students experience.

Conditions in Hispanic Families and Communities. The social and economic status of Hispanic families has an obvious effect on the success of their children in public schools. One basic theme of education research in the United States and elsewhere is the powerful relationship between these family characteristics and school performance. Educational success is influenced dramatically by the preschool years, when extremely important preparation for effective learning takes place, by the educational background of the parents (which is strongly linked to their social and economic status), and by the stability of the family and its ability to provide for the child's basic needs for food, shelter, educational resources, study space, and parental support. We know that children who live in areas with large concentrations of low-income children are likely to attend schools with lower levels of competition, more distractions, less qualified and less experienced teachers, lower expectations, and so on. In low-income schools many students stay no more than a few months before housing and/or job problems force their parents to move them to another school area. It is thus very important to consider these social and economic facts when assessing the problems facing Hispanic schools.

A very large and growing number of Hispanic children are living in poverty, within single-parent families, and attending schools with high proportions of minority and low-income children. More than one-fourth of Hispanic children were living in poverty in 1981, and 67 percent of those living in female-headed families were below the poverty line. Hispanic women who were full-time workers had lower average incomes than either black or white women in 1980 (U.S. Commission on Civil Rights, 1983). By 1986, 28 percent of Hispanic children were in female-headed families (U.S. Bureau of the Census, 1987c).

The higher fertility rate of Hispanic women is likely to have a profound effect on American schools. During 1986, Hispanic women made up 8 percent of the women of childbearing age but had 12 percent of the babies. Fifteen percent of Hispanic women, as opposed to 11 percent of black and 9 percent of white women, reported that they expected to have families of four or more children (U.S. Bureau of the Census, 1987b). The numbers of young Hispanics also continued to grow as a result of the large and continuing immigration.

Single-parent families are the poorest, and statistics show that a substantial fraction of the Hispanic children now in the United States were born to unmarried women in the mid 1980s.

Twenty-three percent of Hispanic children, as opposed to 49 percent of black and 12 percent of white, were born into such households (U.S. Bureau of the Census, 1987b). The severe poverty and low parental education in these families mean that very large numbers of Hispanic children will be coming to school from backgrounds that put them at risk of educational failure. A larger fraction of Hispanic children will be coming to school from households with few resources, and even more will be going into schools where they will be isolated from middle-class Anglo children.

College Enrollment Trends. College administrators are far less worried about declining Hispanic enrollments than about black access to higher education, because the number of Latino students on campus has remained stable or even risen slowly. The number of Hispanic students enrolled in all U.S. institutions of higher education rose from 384,000 in the fall of 1976 to 624,000 in the fall of 1986, an increase of 62 percent ("Gap in Hispanic Test Scores . . . ," 1988). It is only when one compares these figures to the enormous rise in the number of Hispanics in the college-age population that one can understand how apparent progress can mask a dramatic decline in access and choice for college-age Hispanic students.

It is the decline in the access of black high school graduates to college that has received the most attention, because the numbers so obviously declined in many sectors of education. The statistics from the most important sources of national data, the Census Bureau's Current Population Survey, show a much less dramatic trend for Hispanics (Table 3.6). Among high school graduates, these data show that Hispanics (who were far less likely to finish high school than were whites) attended college at a 3 percent higher rate than white graduates in 1976 but were 5 percent less likely than Anglos to be in college in 1986. *p. 50 Table 3.6*

When one adds the differing dropout rates to this deteriorating level of college going among Hispanic high school graduates, the scale of the problem becomes more apparent. Of every 100 young Hispanic adults in 1985, only 59 were high school graduates, and of this number only 29 percent, or 17,

IS CAPT.

Table 3.6. Percentage of Hispanic and Anglo 18-to-24-Year-Old
High School Graduates Enrolled in College, 1976–1986. (Source)

	1976	1978	1980	1982	1984	1986
Hispanics	35.8	27.2	29.9	29.2	29.9	29.4
Whites	32.8	31.3	32.1	33.3	33.9	34.5

R/T

Source: U.S. Bureau of the Census Current Population Reports data,
nos. 77–88; "Table of Civil Rights Statistics," 1988.

were enrolled in college. This compared to a white high school
graduation rate of 84 out of 100 students and a college enrollment rate of 35 percent that would produce 29 collegians. Whites
thus had a 71 percent higher rate of college participation than
Hispanics. This very simple calculation shows how vital it is
for education officials to look beyond the pool of high school
graduates and to probe much more deeply into the issue of
precollege education.

*Declining Proportion of Men in the College-Going Popula-
tion.* American colleges have had a rising share of female and
a declining share of male college students during the last decade.
This change has been particularly sharp among Hispanics.
Hispanic collegians were 55 percent male in 1976, but only 47
percent male in the fall of 1986. Although the percentage of black
male collegians in 1986 was lower (40 percent) than that of
Hispanic males, the drop among Hispanics was faster. Whites
had a small majority of female students. Only the Asian college population remained relatively unchanged at 53 percent
male students ("Table of Civil Rights Statistics," 1988).

    This pattern was very apparent in the college enrollment
data in some of the metropolitan areas that will be examined
later in this chapter. In metropolitan Los Angeles, which has
the largest concentration of Hispanics in the United States, the
clear male majority in the Hispanic college-going population
in the mid 1970s gave way to a clear female majority in the mid
1980s. The much higher high school dropout rate for Hispanic
males reported in a recent Chicago study could help explain this
change. Within the Chicago public schools young men were

dropping out at a 20 percent higher rate than young women (Hess and Lauber, 1985). The same pattern does not appear, however, in the metropolitan Houston data (Paul, 1988).

High School and College Trends
in Three Metropolitan Areas

National data reveal a great deal about the general trends affecting Hispanic students, but a much more sharply focused analysis is needed if the areas of the educational system requiring greatest attention are to be pinpointed. More than nine-tenths of Hispanic public school students live in metropolitan areas, and Hispanics are disproportionately concentrated in the largest central-city school districts. The twenty-five largest city districts contained 30 percent of all U.S. Latino students in the fall of 1986 but only 3 percent of Anglo students (Orfield and Monfort, 1988). Since most Hispanic students are concentrated in the metropolitan areas of a few states, it should be useful to examine trends in several of the largest of these areas. The following data come from the University of Chicago's Metropolitan Opportunity Project analysis of trends in a national study that included metropolitan Los Angeles, Houston, and Chicago, three of the preeminent centers of Hispanic settlement.

Metropolitan Houston. During the 1985–86 school year there were 187,000 students attending high school in the metropolitan Houston region. Twenty-five percent of them were in the Houston Independent School District (HISD), which includes the core of the city of Houston, and 75 percent of them were in outlying districts. During the period from 1970 to 1985, the central-city district's share of the region's high school enrollment had declined from 41 to 25 percent, the district having lost 12,000 students. HISD more than doubled its Hispanic high school enrollment during this period, while white enrollment dropped two-thirds, and black enrollment fell one-sixth from its 1978 peak. In the 1985 school year HISD enrolled 44 percent of the area's Hispanic secondary students, compared to only 11 percent of its white students. Surburban Hispanic high school students were in much better and more highly integrated schools than those in the central district, which had become much more segregated since the 1960s. Eighty-five percent of the HISD Hispanic students were in predominantly minority schools by 1985, and the proportion in intensely segregated, 90 to 100 percent minority schools had increased sevenfold to 36 percent by 1985. Hispanics also accounted for one-ninth of suburban high school enrollment by 1985. In contrast to the central-city Hispanic students, who attended schools with an average enrollment that was half Hispanic, their suburban counterparts were typically in schools where only one-fifth of the students were Hispanic and only one-eighth were black. The typical Hispanic suburban student attended a high school that was 67 percent white. Hispanic students in different parts of metropolitan Houston are thus having very different educational experiences. Those in the city are in a situation similar to the situation that urban blacks often face, while those in the suburbs are being educated and socialized in a predominantly white middle-class world.

Metropolitan Chicago. All levels of metropolitan Chicago education have experienced a large increase in Hispanic students in recent years. Hispanic enrollment increased in the Chicago public schools from 10 percent to 20 percent between 1971 and 1981. During the same period, the suburban Hispanic proportion doubled from 2 to 4 percent while Latino enrollment in the Catholic schools of the Chicago Archdiocese, which has the nation's largest parochial system, doubled from 8 to 16 percent. Hispanic enrollment in the area's schools was soaring, while white and black enrollments were declining. These trends continued in the 1980s (Orfield and Tostado, 1983).

The 1980 census showed that Hispanics had lower levels of education than blacks or whites, as well as lower levels of college completion in all major sections of metropolitan Chicago. Within the city, most Hispanics had only a grade school education and only one in twenty had a college degree. In the secondary settlements in the satellite cities around Chicago, blacks were half again as likely to have college degrees as were Hispanics, and whites were more than three times as likely to have degrees. There were strong links between level of education and employment and income for Chicago area Latinos (Orfield and Tostado, 1983). In the metropolitan Chicago area, 6 percent of Hispanics, 8 percent of blacks, and 20 percent of whites had college degrees in 1980. Latinos lagged behind blacks in all areas with significant minority populations, but Latinos in the suburbs were nearly twice as likely as those in the city to have college degrees (Orfield and others, 1984).

In 1980, Hispanics made up 10 percent of metropolitan Chicago's population aged eighteen to twenty-four, 4.4 percent of the college enrollment, and 2.9 percent of those receiving B.A. degrees. The number of B.A. degrees received that year represented a 17 percent increase from the number awarded five years earlier, but the increase was much less than the growth in Hispanic college-age population during the five years. Hispanics who enrolled in college were substantially less likely to finish than either blacks or whites (Orfield and others, 1984).

Hispanic students in metropolitan Chicago were concentrated in the city and in a limited number of the eighty-five suburban districts that had high schools. Although a much smaller share of the Hispanic students attended schools in suburban areas, there were sharp differences between the city and the suburban experiences for students. Hispanic students living in the city of Chicago in 1986 were in schools where the average minority composition was 79 percent, while their suburban counterparts, much like those in metro Houston, were in schools with an average of 71 percent white students.

In the metropolitan Chicago area there was a very strong relationship between the percent of minority students and the percent of low-income students. The correlation between the percent of black and Hispanic students in a high school in metropolitan Chicago and the percentage of low-income students was a staggering .93. The relationship between percent minority and graduation rate was − .83. Many fewer students at heavily minority schools took college entrance exams. There was a negative .47 correlation coefficient between percent minority in a high school and percent taking the tests. Even though many fewer minority students took the tests, their average scores were dramatically lower than those of white students. The correlation between percent black and Hispanic and average college admissions test scores of metro Chicago high schools was − .92. Further analysis suggested that it was income rather than race that was most powerfully related to these outcomes, but there was such an extremely high relationship between the income level of students attending a school and its racial composition that to talk about one was to talk about the other. There were no predominantly low-income white high schools, for example, and no all middle-class black or Hispanic schools (Garrett, 1987).

When studied simply in terms of the percent of Hispanic students in a school, the relationships were less overwhelming. On a metropolitan level, the correlation between percent Hispanic and percent poor was .28, the correlation with graduation rate was − .40, and the correlation with college entrance scores was − .43 (Garrett, 1987). Many central-city Hispanics, however, were in schools with two disadvantaged minorities.

Within Chicago, as in Houston, segregation of Hispanic students has increased substantially, but the rate of change has been much more rapid in Chicago. In 1970 the typical Chicago Hispanic student was in a 50 percent white school. By 1983, he was in an 83 percent minority school. On a metropolitan level, in 1984, the typical Hispanic student attended a 79.5 percent minority school. Given the relationship between race, class, and all academic outcomes, this trend meant that a larger and larger majority of Hispanic students were attending schools where there were few white or middle-class students, where the dropout rate was very high, and where the level of college preparation was wholly inadequate (Farley and Wurdock, 1979; Weinberg, 1983).

Comparisons of city and suburban schools in the metropolitan Chicago region showed that they were unequal in ways that could directly affect college preparation. The city schools had teachers from much less competitive colleges and many fewer counselors per thousand students, even though minority students, unlike whites, told survey researchers that they relied primarily on school officials for advice about college. A number of virtually all-minority inner-city high schools lacked basic precollegiate courses such as physics and foreign language (Orfield and others, 1984). In other words, not only were minority students segregated in schools with much greater rates of dropouts and much lower test scores, but even the motivated and talented students at these schools were put at a disadvantage by the loss of vital precollegiate resources and opportunities. This analysis does not imply, of course, that the scores of Hispanic and other students would be equal if they were in equally demanding schools, since achievement is affected by many factors, but it does show that equally talented Hispanic students are usually offered systematically inferior educational challenges and opportunities.

Los Angeles High Schools. The patterns reported in Houston and Chicago have strong parallels in Los Angeles. An analysis of data from all schools in California in the mid 1970s showed very strong statewide relationships between percent minority, poverty, and test scores (Espinosa and Ochoa, 1986). A study of patterns in the high schools of the greater Los Angeles area between 1975 and 1985 by researchers at the University of Chicago also found very strong relationships of this sort. These basic relationships were confirmed by a reanalysis of the data by a University of California, Berkeley, research team, which disputed findings about the effects of recent state reforms but confirmed the basic relationship (Jaeger, 1987; Policy Analysis for California Education (PACE), 1988).

The metropolitan Los Angeles research showed a high and rapidly intensifying level of segregation for Hispanics in each county in this area, which has the nation's largest Hispanic settlement. With about a twentieth of the nation's population and about 740,000, or 18 percent, of the nation's Hispanic students, this region had witnessed the rapidly increasing isolation of Hispanics in each of its three major areas. Between 1970 and 1984, the number of whites in the schools of typical Latino students dropped from 45 percent to 17 percent in Los Angeles County, from 73 percent to 31 percent in Orange County, and from 63 percent to 40 percent in the Riverside and San Bernadino County area (DBS Corporation, 1987; Orfield, Monfort, and George, 1987).

Data from the 1984–85 school year show that the correlation between the percent black and Hispanic and average math scores in metropolitan Los Angeles high schools was – .88. The relationship was even stronger for reading, – .90, and only slightly weaker for writing, – .85. The relationships with percent of white students were similarly strong in the opposite direction. When only the percent of Hispanic students in a school was considered, the relationships were less overwhelming but still very substantial, from – .53 to – .58 (Jaeger, 1987). Segregated minority schools, in other words, were experiencing very severe educational problems, and the number of such schools and the intensity of their isolation were rapidly increasing. These data do not, of course, show that segregation causes inequality in education generally, but it does show that Hispanic students tend to be concentrated in schools where the tone and the level of instruction are set by large proportions of poorly prepared students.

Declining College Access for Hispanics in Four Metropolitan Areas. National statistics report that the percent of new Hispanic high school graduates enrolling in college the next academic year dropped from its peak of 53 percent, recorded in 1976 and 1980, to 44 percent in the fall of 1986. During the same period the enrollment rate for Anglo graduates was rising (U.S. Department of Education, Center for Education Statistics, 1988b). Recent data on four metropolitan areas also show serious declines in the proportion of Hispanic high school seniors going on to college and indicate that those who do make it to college are increasingly concentrated in community colleges from which few students successfully transfer and receive a B.A. degree (see Table 3.7). Moreover, the Chicago and Houston data clearly show that there is a growing gap between the graduation rates of those Hispanics and Anglos who have enrolled in various kinds of colleges in recent years. The data show, in other words, a decline in access to college, a restricted set of choices, and increased attrition within college for Hispanics.

The Metropolitan Opportunity Project data from metropolitan Los Angeles, Chicago, Houston, and Philadelphia include

IS CAPT

Table 3.7. Total Four-Year Hispanic College Enrollment
as a Percentage of 12th-Grade Enrollment in Selected Metropolitan Areas. *(Source)*

	1980	1984
Chicago	102.1	79.7
Houston	75.9	66.4
Los Angeles	58.1	46.0
Philadelphia	39.0	34.3

R/T

Source: Orfield and Paul, 1987–88.

year-by-year high school and college racial statistics. They show
us exactly how many students are in school, how many are
graduating, and what schools and colleges they are in. They
show the changing relationship between finishing high school
and beginning college for Hispanic students, and the changing
kinds of concentrations of Hispanics in various colleges. These
data make it clear that access to college has declined even more
sharply for Hispanic high school graduates than for their black
counterparts.

There has been a notable decline in degree attainment
ratios among Hispanics enrolled in four-year colleges in most
of these metropolitan areas between 1980 and 1984. In Chicago
the decline was 2.3 percent, in Houston the drop was 10.9 percent, and in metropolitan Los Angeles 0.4 percent. Only in
Philadelphia was there a slight increase of 1.1 percent, from a
very low level. The underlying trend is toward greater inequality
for Hispanics, even for those who make it to college.

Conclusion

The numbers of Hispanics of school and college age are
increasing very rapidly in the United States, so rapidly that both
research and policy are running far behind the demographic
changes. These changes are likely to continue well into the future.
If they do, Hispanic students will become the nation's largest
minority group but at the same time will be highly disadvantaged
educationally. If the existing trends continue, Hispanics will be increasingly concentrated in low-income minority schools with poor

records of graduation and achievement. Although they will represent a continually growing share of the college-age population, particularly in those states where they live in the largest numbers, there will be an increasingly severe mismatch between their academic preparation and the rising admissions requirements of many colleges. There is a clear need for major efforts to break the cycle of growing inequality for Latinos in both high schools and colleges.

---

note → [1] *The data:* Much of the analysis here is built on federal and state school and college enrollment statistics rather than on population data. These data have powerful advantages over census statistics for analyzing the dynamics of Hispanic population growth and changes in school and college enrollment and achievement patterns. The Hispanic community is changing extremely rapidly, and school statistics are reported annually on state and local, as well as national, levels. Census statistics, unlike school data, do not report whites, blacks, and Hispanics as mutually exclusive categories. In general, a lack of consistent definitions across time makes it difficult to do any detailed analysis of trends using census data. It also means that every time Hispanics are compared with census "whites," the "white" part of the comparison includes millions of Hispanics, and so the comparisons understate the real differences between the two groups. For most policy purposes, the most useful comparisons are with non-Hispanic whites or blacks. There has been a consistent definition of Hispanics ever since school and college enrollment statistics were first collected nationally by federal civil rights officials.

Many of the year-by-year estimates of changes in high school graduation and college-going rates in this report come from the U.S. Census Bureau's Current Population Surveys, which survey about 59,500 households with a response rate of approximately 96 percent. One problem with this data set, according to the Census Bureau, is that there is undercoverage of some categories, particularly males and minorities. In addition, the statistical adjustment techniques used in calculating the national numbers do not adjust for the known undercount of Hispanics in the 1980 census, which is used as a baseline (U.S. Bureau of the Census, 1987a).

Hispanic students rely overwhelmingly on public schools. Data from the National Catholic Education Association on the enrollment of Hispanic students in Catholic elementary and secondary schools show that Catholic schools enroll a small and shrinking share of this economically disadvantaged and largely Catholic population. In the 1987–88 school year there were just over a quarter million (256,000) Hispanic students in Catholic grade schools, representing about one-eighth of the total enrollment in these schools. The Catholic school system as a whole has declined by almost half during this period, so that Hispanics in fact constituted a growing share of a declining system. Although the number of Hispanic students in Catholic schools grew by about one-fifth from the fall of 1971 to the fall of 1987, the increase in their enrollment in public schools over the same sixteen-year period was approximately four times as fast. Thus a growing share of the total Hispanic enrollment attended public schools. Only about 6 percent of Hispanic elementary students now attend Catholic schools.

(Hardpan)

The effect of Catholic education is even more limited at the high school level. In 1980 there were only 58,800 Hispanic students in Catholic high schools (National Catholic Education Association, 1988; U.S. Department of Education, 1986). The limited size and substantial tuition of Catholic high schools discourage all but a few Hispanic students from attending them. RH

p.59

References

Arias, M. B. "The Context of Education for Hispanic Students: An Overview." *American Journal of Education,* 1986, *95,* 26–57.

DBS Corporation. "1986 Elementary and Secondary School Civil Rights Survey: National and State Summary of Projected Data." n.d. (Undated computer printouts.)

DBS Corporation. "Comparison of Exposure Rates and Desegregation Indices: Years 1970 and 1980." Office for Civil Rights, U.S. Department of Education, Aug. 1982.

DBS Corporation. "1986 Elementary and Secondary School Civil Rights Survey, National Summaries." Office for Civil Rights, U.S. Department of Education, Dec. 1987.

Espinosa, R., and Ochoa, A. "Concentration of California Hispanic Students in Schools with Low Achievement: A Research Note." *American Journal of Education,* 1986, *95,* 77–95.

Farley, R., and Wurdock, C. "School Integration and Enrollment in the Nation's Largest Cities: An Analysis of Recent Trends." Proceedings of the Social Statistics Section of the American Statistical Association, 1979.

"Florida Supplants Pennsylvania as Fourth Most Popular State Behind California, New York, and Texas." *New York Times,* Dec. 30, 1987, Sec. 2, p. 9.

"Gap in Hispanic Test Scores Links Income, Curriculum." *Education Week,* Mar. 9, 1988, p. 3.

Garrett, J. "Metropolitan Chicago Public High Schools: Race, Poverty, and Educational Opportunity." University of Chicago Metropolitan Opportunity Project, Report no. 5, July 1987.

Hess, G. A., Jr., and Lauber, D. *Drop Outs from the Chicago Schools.* Chicago: Chicago Panel on Public School Final, Apr. 1985.

Jaeger, C. "Minority and Low-Income High Schools: Evidence of Educational Inequality in Metro Los Angeles." University of Chicago Metropolitan Opportunity Project, Report no. 8, Oct. 1987.

National Catholic Education Association, *Statistical Report on Schools, Enrollment, and Staffing, 1987–88.* Washington, D.C.: National Catholic Education Association, 1988.

Orfield, G., and Monfort, F. *Racial Change and Desegregation in Large School Districts, 1968–1986.* Alexandria, Va.: National School Boards Association, 1988.

Orfield, G., Monfort, F., and George, R. "School Segregation in the 1980s, Trends in the United States and Metropolitan Areas." Report to the Joint Center for Political Studies, July 1987.

Orfield, G., and Paul, F. "Declines in Minority Access: A Tale of Five Cities." *Educational Record,* Fall 1987–Winter 1988, pp. 57–62.

Orfield, G., and Tostado, R. (eds.). *Latinos in Metropolitan Chicago.* Chicago: Latino Institute, 1983.

Orfield, G., and others. *The Chicago Study of Access and Choice in Higher Education.* Chicago: University of Chicago Committee on Public Policy Studies, 1984.

Paul, F. "Declining Minority Access to College in Metropolitan Chicago, 1975–1985." University of Chicago Metropolitan Opportunity Project, Report no. 2, Jan. 1987a.

Paul, F. "Declining Minority Access to College in Metropolitan Philadelphia, 1976–1984." University of Chicago Metropolitan Opportunity Project, Report no. 3, Apr. 1987b.

Paul, F. "Declining Minority Access to College in Metropolitan Houston, 1976–1986." University of Chicago Metropolitan Opportunity Project, Report no. 16, Oct. 1988.

Policy Analysis for California Education (PACE). *Conditions of Education in California 1988.* Policy paper no. 88-3-2. Berkeley: School of Education, University of California, Mar. 1988.

"Population Mark Is Seen for Texas: Census Bureau Says the State Will Push New York Out of Second Place by 1995." *New York Times,* Aug. 4, 1988, p. 11.

"Table of Civil Rights Statistics." *Chronicle of Higher Education,* Mar. 9, 1988, p. A36.

U.S Bureau of the Census. *Educational Attainment in the United States: March 1982 to 1985.* Current Population Reports, Series P-20, no. 415. Washington, D.C.: U.S. Government Printing Office, 1987a.

U.S. Bureau of the Census. *Fertility of American Women: June 1986.* Current Population Reports, Series P-20, no. 421. Washington, D.C.: U.S. Government Printing Office, 1987b.

U.S. Bureau of the Census. *Marital Status and Living Arrangements: March 1986.* Current Population Reports, Series P-20, no. 418. Washington, D.C.: U.S. Government Printing Office, 1987c.

U.S. Commission on Civil Rights. *A Growing Crisis: Disadvantaged Women and Their Children.* Washington, D.C.: U.S. Government Printing Office, May 1983.

U.S. Department of Education, Center for Education Statistics. *Digest of Education Statistics: 1988.* Washington, D.C.: U.S. Government Printing Office, 1988.

U.S. Department of Education, Center for Education Statistics. "Trends in Minority Enrollment in Higher Education, Fall 1976–Fall 1986." *Survey Report,* April 1988b.

Weinberg, M. *The Search for Quality Integrated Education: Policy and Research on Minority Students in School and College.* Westport, Conn.: Greenwood Press, 1983.

E/o Chap. 3

 4

Blacks

by *Gail E. Thomas (SP)* and
Deborah J. Hirsch (SP)

In the 1960s and 1970s, the right of blacks to advance educationally and socially was primarily debated as an ethical issue that struck at the heart of the U.S. Constitution and a "free" democratic society. However, in the forthcoming decade, the educational and social advancement of minorities must be viewed as a national vested interest issue that cuts at the core and basic welfare of the U.S. economy.

By the year 2000, blacks will constitute a 10 percent larger share of the U.S. labor market pool. Employment rates and labor force participation rates are strongly correlated with educational attainment for both minorities and whites. However, for minorities especially, college completion has a direct impact on their employability (College Board, 1985). Thus, it will be imperative for colleges and universities, as well as future employers, to provide quality education and adequate training that will enable minority groups to help meet the needs of the future labor market.

In this chapter we will assess the challenges that lie ahead for blacks in higher education and society in general, but first we will provide an overview of some historical and demographic forces, as well as some current trends, that have shaped the participation of blacks in higher education, which is a matter of essential national policy critical to maintaining the labor base and keeping America competitive.

Historical Background

Educational attainment, especially beyond a high school diploma, constitutes the major avenue for the upward mobility of blacks (as well as for other underrepresented minorities). Historically, blacks were denied opportunities for educational advancement. Before the Civil War, when the slave plantation economy represented the status quo, blacks were legally prohibited from becoming educated at any level. While there were a few attempts by free blacks to establish their own schools, these attempts were limited and had no real impact.

After the war, the Freedmen's Bureau and various black communities and churches, as well as northern philanthropists, established schools that became the foundation of a separate education system for blacks. These schools provided, for the most part, a primary or secondary education rather than a postsecondary education. Gradually, however, they developed college-level courses and then programs to educate black teachers and professionals. According to the 1915 federal survey of black schools, there were thirty-three black colleges enrolling about 2,600 students who were doing some college-level work, though most were studying at the elementary or secondary level. Of these institutions, only Howard University, Meharry Medical College, and Fisk University could be described as postsecondary institutions. It was in these schools that blacks were supposed to receive, through a Supreme Court decision, a "separate but equal" education (*Plessy* v. *Ferguson,* 1896). In reality, the colleges developed for blacks were ill equipped in terms of faculty and facilities (Fleming, 1981).

As the demand for a better quality education increased, many blacks expressed concern that black colleges were receiving unequal treatment relative to white colleges. In 1935, the National Association for the Advancement of Colored People (NAACP) legally charged that even if black institutions were treated equally by federal and state government, the doctrine of "separate but equal" violated the constitutional rights of black citizens.

After prolonged and persistent protest by the NAACP and numerous black citizens, the Supreme Court ruled in its favor (that the doctrine of "separate but equal" was unconstitutional) in the 1954 landmark ruling, *Brown* v. *Board of Education of Topeka*. While *Brown* was primarily directed at segregated public elementary and secondary education, it also had implications for higher education since many white colleges opened their doors to blacks as a result of this ruling. Consequently, the number of blacks attending white colleges in the South rose from 3,000 in 1960 to 24,000 in 1965 and to 98,000 in 1970 (Mingle, 1981). Black migration to the North, coupled with the educational provisions of the GI Bill, also substantially increased black enrollment in northern public white colleges. During this time black college enrollment was at its height; it peaked between 1976 and 1978.

Several factors contributed to this rapid growth in black college enrollment: the intervention and subsequent monitoring of black student enrollment progress by the federal government after the *Brown* and the 1973 *Adams* decisions (the latter mandated desegregation of state systems of higher education); expanded financial aid through the college work-study program, educational opportunity grants, and the guaranteed student loan program; the growth of state higher education systems, which primarily entailed the expansion of two-year and community colleges; and an increase in the pool of black high school graduates. Finally, black student and black community protest and civil rights activism also contributed to the increased participation of blacks in higher education and the development of special recruiting efforts and academic support programs to meet the needs of black students (Peterson and others, 1978).

From Progress to Regression

While blacks made substantial progress in higher education enrollment and participation in the early to mid 1970s, existing data suggest that they lost ground in the 1980s. In fact, the 1980s have been called the years of lost opportunity for blacks (Blake, 1987). Blake cites two trends that have undermined the momentum of the late sixties and early seventies. First, the success of the civil rights movement, which helped to bring so many more blacks into the higher education system, may have led to a certain amount of complacency. Black enrollment in the 1980s has shown a steady decline, but because of the increases of the 1970s, the lack of progress on the part of black students largely went unnoticed. Second, the *Baake* case in 1979 brought into question the use of affirmative action policies that were the bedrock of black progress (Blake, 1987).

Other factors that contributed to the decline in black student higher education attainment in the 1980s include a decrease in the amount, variety, and duration of financial aid (for example, financial aid packages were refigured to include more loans and fewer grants) at the same time that the cost of higher education was increasing. The inadequacy of black students' high school preparation is also critical here (Brown, 1987). Black students take fewer advanced mathematics and science courses and earn lower grades in these courses than whites (Sells, 1976; Brown, 1987; Western Interstate Commission for Higher Education, 1987). Moreover, minority students are more often placed in vocational courses or tracks that do not lead to college and with teachers who have lower expectations for their academic achievement (College Board, 1985).

Despite these obstacles, the number of black students dropping out of high school declined significantly between 1975 and 1985. The percentage of blacks who dropped out of high school fell from 27 percent in 1975 to 17 percent in 1985 (U.S. Bureau of the Census, 1984). But even though more black students are graduating from high school, the number who enroll in college has decreased since 1976. While the percentage of black high school graduates increased from 67.5 percent to 75.6 percent from 1976 to 1985, the percentage of this age cohort among blacks who enrolled in college decreased from 33.5 percent in 1976 to 28 percent in 1981 and dropped again to 26.1 percent in 1985. Similarly, while the proportion of eighteen- to twenty-four-year-old blacks enrolled in college was 22.6 percent in 1976, their percentage had declined to 19.9 percent by 1980 and to 19.8 percent by 1985 (Table 4.1). *pp 66 +67 Table 4.1*

The reason typically cited for the gap between the number of blacks who graduate from high school and the number who enroll in college is that blacks choose other alternatives to college;

IS CAPT.

Table 4.1. High School Completion and College Entrance Rates for Population 18 to 24 Years Old, by Race/Ethnicity: United States, Selected Years (in Thousands). (Source)

	1971	1976	1981	1985
Total:				
Total population 18–24-year-olds	23,668	26,919	28,965	27,122
Number completing high school	18,691	21,677	23,343	22,349
Number enrolled in college	6,210	7,181	7,575	7,537
High school graduates as a percentage of total	79.0%	80.5%	80.6%	82.4%
College entrants as a percentage of 18–24-year-old high school graduates	33.2%	33.1%	32.5%	33.7%
College entrants as a percentage of 18–24-year-old population	26.2%	26.7%	26.2%	27.8%
White:				
Total population white 18–24-year-olds	20,533	23,119	24,486	22,632
Number completing high school	16,693	19,045	20,123	18,916
Number enrolled in college	5,594	6,276	6,549	6,500
High school graduates as a percentage of total	81.3%	82.4%	82.2%	83.6%
College entrants as a percentage of 18–24-year-old high school graduates	33.5%	33.0%	32.5%	34.4%
College entrants as a percentage of 18–24-year-old population	27.2%	27.1%	26.7%	28.7%
Percentage of the total 18–24-year-old population	86.6%	85.9%	84.5%	83.4%
Black:				
Total population black 18–24-year-olds	2,866	3,315	3,778	3,716
Number completing high school	1,789	2,239	2,678	2,810
Number enrolled in college	522	749	750	734
High school graduates as a percentage of total	62.4%	67.5%	70.9%	75.6%
College entrants as a percentage of 18–24-year-old high school graduates	29.2%	33.5%	28.0%	26.1%
College entrants as a percentage of 18–24-year-old population	18.2%	22.6%	19.9%	19.8%
Percentage of the total 18–24-year-old population	12.1%	12.3%	13.4%	13.7%
Hispanic:				
Total population Hispanic 18–24-year-olds	1,338	1,551	2,052	2,221
Number completing high school	694	862	1,144	1,396
Number enrolled in college	179	309	342	375

Table 4.1. High School Completion and College Entrance Rates
for Population 18 to 24 Years Old, by Race/Ethnicity:
United States, Selected Years (in Thousands), Cont'd.

High school graduates as a percentage of total	51.9%	55.6%	55.8%	62.9%
College entrants as a percentage of 18–24-year-old high school graduates	25.8%	35.8%	29.8%	26.9%
College entrants as a percentage of 18–24-year-old population	13.4%	19.9%	16.6%	16.9%
Percentage of the total 18–24-year-old population	5.6%	5.7%	7.1%	8.2%

Note: Since these high school completion rates were calculated by adding the numbers of individuals in this age group enrolled in college as of October of that year and the number of high school graduates not enrolled in college, these rates include individuals who enrolled in college without receiving a high school diploma or a GED. Several states do not require entering junior college students to have a diploma or GED. Therefore, these high school completion rates will be slightly higher than figures that do not include this relatively small population.

ªHispanics may be of any race.

Source: Based on U.S. Department of Commerce, Bureau of the Census, Current Population Reports, Series P-20, 247, 309, 373, and 409, as compiled in American Council on Education, 1987b.

more blacks are typically found in vocational-technical schools, and a higher proportion of blacks are also found in the military (American Council on Education, 1987b). While some suggest that more blacks choose to go to work instead of college, the unemployment figures for blacks in this age group disprove this view (American Council on Education, 1987b). The decrease in black student enrollment has also been linked, in part, to the decline in affirmative action legislation and programs in the 1980s (Blackwell, 1987; Copeland, 1984; Thomas, 1987). The federal ruling to dismiss the *Adams* case, which sought to redress unequal educational quality in predominantly black and white public institutions, provides a legitimate basis for concern over the future status of blacks in American higher education.

While blacks enrolled in college in increasing numbers from 1976 to 1986 (Table 4.2), the proportion of black students enrolled declined from 9.4 percent of all students in 1976 to 8.6 percent in 1986. Black enrollments, like white enrollments, were

Table 4.2. Total Enrollment in Institutions of Higher Education, by Control of Institution and Race/Ethnicity and Sex of Student: Biennally, Fall 1976 to Fall 1986. (source)

Control of Institution and Race/Ethnicity and Sex of Student	Number, in Thousands						Percent Distribution					
	1976	1978	1980	1982	1984	1986	1976	1978	1980	1982	1984	1986
All Institutions												
Total	10,986	11,231	12,087	12,388	12,235	12,501	100.0	100.0	100.0	100.0	100.0	100.0
White, non-Hispanic	9,076	9,194	9,833	9,997	9,815	9,914	82.6	81.9	81.4	80.7	80.2	79.3
Black, non-Hispanic	1,033	1,054	1,107	1,101	1,076	1,081	9.4	9.4	9.2	8.9	8.8	8.6
Hispanic	384	417	472	519	535	624	3.5	3.7	3.9	4.2	4.4	5.0
Asian or Pacific Islander	198	235	286	351	390	448	1.8	2.1	2.4	2.8	3.2	3.6
American Indian/Alaskan Native	76	78	84	88	84	90	0.7	0.7	0.7	0.7	0.7	0.7
Nonresident alien	219	253	305	331	335	344	2.0	2.2	2.5	2.7	2.7	2.7
Public												
Total	8,641	8,770	9,456	9,695	9,458	9,722	78.7	78.1	78.2	78.3	77.3	77.8
White, non-Hispanic	7,095	7,136	7,656	7,785	7,543	7,650	64.6	63.5	63.3	62.8	61.6	61.2
Black, non-Hispanic	831	840	876	873	844	855	7.6	7.5	7.2	7.0	6.9	6.8
Hispanic	337	363	406	446	456	539	3.1	3.2	3.4	3.6	3.7	4.3
Asian or Pacific Islander	166	195	240	296	323	372	1.5	1.7	2.0	2.4	2.6	3.0
American Indian/Alaskan Native	68	68	74	77	72	79	0.6	0.6	0.6	0.6	0.6	0.6
Nonresident alien	145	167	204	219	219	226	1.3	1.5	1.7	1.8	1.8	1.8

Private

Total	2,345	2,461	2,630	2,693	2,777	2,779	21.3	21.9	21.8	21.7	22.7	22.2
White, non-Hispanic	1,982	2,058	2,177	2,212	2,272	2,264	18.0	18.3	18.0	17.9	18.6	18.1
Black, non-Hispanic	202	215	231	228	232	226	1.8	1.9	1.9	1.8	1.9	1.8
Hispanic	47	55	66	74	79	84	0.4	0.5	0.5	0.6	0.6	0.7
Asian or Pacific Islander	32	40	47	55	67	76	0.3	0.4	0.4	0.4	0.5	0.6
AmericanIndian/Alaskan Native	9	9	10	10	11	11	0.1	0.1	0.1	0.1	0.1	0.1
Nonresident alien	73	85	101	113	116	118	0.7	0.8	0.8	0.9	0.9	0.9

Men

Total	5,794	5,621	5,868	5,999	5,859	5,885	52.7	50.1	48.5	48.4	47.9	47.1
White, non-Hispanic	4,814	4,613	4,773	4,830	4,690	4,646	43.8	41.1	39.5	39.0	38.3	37.2
Black, non-Hispanic	470	453	464	458	437	436	4.3	4.0	3.8	3.7	3.6	3.5
Hispanic	210	213	232	252	254	292	1.9	1.9	1.9	2.0	2.1	2.3
Asian or Pacific Islander	108	126	151	189	210	239	1.0	1.1	1.3	1.5	1.7	1.9
American Indian/Alaskan Native	39	37	38	40	38	40	0.4	0.3	0.3	0.3	0.3	0.3
Nonresident alien	154	180	211	230	231	232	1.4	1.6	1.7	1.9	1.9	1.9

Women

Total	5,191	5,609	6,219	6,389	6,376	6,615	47.3	49.9	51.5	51.6	52.1	52.9
White, non-Hispanic	4,262	4,581	5,060	5,167	5,125	5,268	38.8	40.8	41.9	41.7	41.9	42.1
Black, non-Hispanic	563	601	643	644	639	645	5.1	5.4	5.3	5.2	5.2	5.2
Hispanic	174	205	240	267	281	332	1.6	1.8	2.0	2.2	2.3	2.7
Asian or Pacific Islander	89	109	135	162	180	209	0.8	1.0	1.1	1.3	1.5	1.7
American Indian/Alaskan Native	38	41	46	48	46	51	0.3	0.4	0.4	0.4	0.4	0.4
Nonresident alien	65	73	94	101	104	111	0.6	0.7	0.8	0.8	0.9	0.9

Note: Because of underreporting and nonreporting of racial/ethnic data, data were estimated when possible. Also, due to rounding, detail may not add to totals.

Source: U.S. Department of Education, Center for Education Statistics, 1988.

concentrated in public rather than private institutions, but black students were more likely to be enrolled in two-year institutions. This has serious implications for minority degree attainment since students at two-year institutions are more likely to drop out of college and less likely to earn bachelor's degrees or enter graduate or professional schools (Brown, 1987). *pp. 68 & 69 - Table 4.2*

p. 70   The trends in degree attainment for blacks have followed the downward pattern in enrollment (Table 4.3). The proportion of blacks who received bachelor's degrees declined between 1976 (6.5 percent) and 1984 (5.9 percent). And while the proportion of blacks who enrolled in graduate school declined from 5.9 percent in 1976 to 5 percent in 1986, professional school enrollments for blacks increased from 4.6 percent in 1976 to 5.2 percent in 1986. The number of doctoral degrees awarded to blacks decreased from 4.3 percent in 1976 to 4.1 percent in 1984 (Brown, 1987; Thomas, 1987; Blackwell, 1987). Data on graduate degrees awarded to blacks from 1976 to 1984 indicate a transition from the fields of education and the social sciences to the fields of business and administration, areas that lead to immediate employment opportunities rather than further education. *Table 4.3 on pp. 72 & 73*

Demographic and Socioeconomic Trends

In order to understand what the future holds for black students in higher education, one needs to look at the larger demographic and socioeconomic picture of blacks in this country. The black population has been growing considerably faster than the total U.S. population. In 1980, blacks represented 11.8 percent of the total U.S. population; they increased to 12.2 percent in 1987 and can be expected to grow to 13.1 percent by the year 2000 (U.S. Bureau of the Census, 1984). These numbers suggest that a younger black population, in its prime childbearing years, will produce a significant proportion of the school population for several decades to come. In 1987, the median age for blacks was 27.2 years as compared with 33 years for whites. This six-year difference has remained fairly constant since the 1970s.

Although the historical trend was for southern blacks to migrate north, this was reversed during the latter half of the 1970s, when more blacks returned to the South than left. In 1980, 53 percent of the black population in the U.S. was living in the South. Today more than half of the black population is still located in the Sun Belt, and the other half is concentrated in ten states in the Northeast, Midwest, and California. In 1980 most blacks (58 percent) were also living in central cities. This represented a 13 percent increase from the 1970s, but this rise was much less than the 32 percent increase that occurred during the 1960s. Even though the proportion of blacks residing outside the central cities grew by 43 percent in the 1970s, in 1980 blacks still made up only 6 percent of the total population residing outside of central cities. Thus it is clear that educational opportunities for blacks in the South and in urban areas will remain particularly important.

The U.S. Census Bureau, in an April 1, 1988, press release, predicted that by the year 2000 the black population will total 35 million, an increase of 16 percent, while whites will total 222.1 million, an increase of 7 percent. Most of the black population growth from 1988 to the year 2000 will be in five states: 3.2 million will be in New York, 2.9 million in California, 2.4 million in Texas, 2.3 million in Florida, and 2.2 million in Georgia.

By the year 2000 blacks will total about 19 percent of the total population in the South as compared with 12 percent in the Northeast, 11 percent in the Midwest, and 6 percent in the West. Census Bureau projections also indicate that the following states will have populations that are at least one-fourth black: the District of Columbia (68 percent), Mississippi (36 percent), Louisiana (32 percent), South Carolina (30 percent), Maryland (28 percent), Georgia (27 percent), and Alabama (26 percent). If these areas are to achieve their economic development goals, they must educate their minorities so that they can become contributing members of society rather than a burden on it.

pp. 72 + 73 contain Table 4.3 which has been described.

p. 74 **Black Family Earnings and Household Structures.** The income for all black families has continued to lag behind that of

Table 4.3. Total Enrollment in Institutions of Higher Education, by Level of Study and Race/Ethnicity of Student: Biennally, Fall 1976 to Fall 1986. (source)

Level of Study and Race/Ethnicity of Student	Number, in Thousands						Percent Distribution by Level of Study					
	1976	1978	1980	1982	1984	1986	1976	1978	1980	1982	1984	1986
Undergraduate Enrollment												
Total	9,520	9,757	10,560	10,875	10,610	10,797	100.0	100.0	100.0	100.0	100.0	100.0
White, non-Hispanic	7,827	7,946	8,556	8,749	8,484	8,552	82.2	81.4	81.0	80.5	80.0	79.2
Total minority	1,550	1,642	1,797	1,907	1,911	2,041	16.3	16.8	17.0	17.5	18.0	18.9
Black, non-Hispanic	950	975	1,028	1,028	995	995	10.0	10.0	9.7	9.4	9.4	9.2
Hispanic	357	388	438	485	495	569	3.7	4.0	4.1	4.5	4.7	5.3
Asian or Pacific Islander	173	206	253	313	343	394	1.8	2.1	2.4	2.9	3.2	3.6
American Indian/Alaskan Native	70	72	79	82	78	84	0.7	0.7	0.7	0.8	0.7	0.8
Nonresident alien	142	169	208	220	216	204	1.5	1.7	2.0	2.0	2.0	1.9
Graduate Enrollment												
Total	1,221	1,219	1,250	1,235	1,344	1,434	100.0	100.0	100.0	100.0	100.0	100.0
White, non-Hispanic	1,030	1,019	1,030	1,002	1,087	1,132	84.3	83.6	82.4	81.1	80.9	78.9
Total minority	119	120	125	123	141	166	9.8	9.8	10.0	10.0	10.5	11.6
Black, non-Hispanic	72	68	66	61	67	72	5.9	5.6	5.3	4.9	5.0	5.0
Hispanic	22	24	27	27	32	46	1.8	1.9	2.2	2.2	2.4	3.2
Asian or Pacific Islander	21	24	28	30	37	43	1.7	2.0	2.2	2.5	2.8	3.0
American Indian/Alaskan Native	4	4	4	5	5	5	0.4	0.4	0.4	0.4	0.4	0.4
Nonresident alien	73	80	94	108	115	136	6.0	6.6	7.5	8.8	8.6	9.5

First-Professional Enrollment

	244	255	277	278	278	270	100.0	100.0	100.0	100.0	100.0	100.0
Total	244	255	277	278	278	270	100.0	100.0	100.0	100.0	100.0	100.0
White, non-Hispanic	220	229	248	246	243	230	90.1	89.8	89.5	88.5	87.4	85.2
Total minority	21	22	26	29	32	36	8.6	8.6	9.5	10.4	11.4	13.2
Black, non-Hispanic	11	11	13	13	13	14	4.6	4.3	4.6	4.7	4.8	5.2
Hispanic	5	5	7	7	8	9	1.9	2.0	2.4	2.5	2.9	3.4
Asian or Pacific Islander	4	5	6	8	9	11	1.7	2.0	2.2	2.9	3.4	4.2
American Indian/Alaskan Native	1	1	1	1	1	1	0.5	0.4	0.3	0.4	0.4	0.4
Nonresident alien	3	3	3	3	3	4	1.3	1.2	1.0	1.1	1.2	1.5

Note: Because of underreporting and nonreporting of racial/ethnic data, data were estimated when possible. Also, due to rounding, detail may not add to totals.

Source: U.S. Department of Education, Center for Education Statistics, 1988.

the total U.S. population. Black family income was only 60 percent of the median income of white families in 1971 and has remained at about 56 percent of that of white families since 1981 (Matney and Johnson, 1984). Moreover, according to a report by the Census Bureau, the average monthly income of blacks lags behind whites at almost every level of educational attainment. Only at the master's degree level was there no significant difference between the incomes of blacks and whites; at the doctoral and professional degree levels, the small sample sizes precluded any comparisons (U.S. Bureau of the Census, 1984).

The decline in black family median income is partly attributable to the increase in the proportion of black families headed by single females. While this in turn is partly due to an increase in divorce, about one-third of all black single families are headed by women who have never been married. Less than half (41 percent) of all black children lived with both parents in 1982; 49 percent lived with one parent (usually the mother), and 8 percent lived with neither parent (Matney and Johnson, 1984).

In 1982, about 41 percent of the female-headed households in the United States (2.6 million) were found among blacks (Matney and Johnson, 1984). This represented an increase of 13 percent among blacks since 1970 (College Board, 1985). In contrast, the number of white female-headed households increased by only 3 percent during this time. The median income for these single families in 1981 ($7,510) was about 38 percent of the median income of black married-couple households ($19,620). In 1987, the median income for black single families ($9,710) was about 36 percent of that of married-couple households ($27,180). The decline in the number of black married-couple households as a proportion of all black families resulted in a considerable reduction in earnings for blacks.

Poverty and Unemployment. Black female-headed households accounted for 70 percent of all poor black families in 1981 (Matney and Johnson, 1984). The number of blacks with incomes below the poverty level increased from 7.5 million in 1970 to 9.2 million in 1981 and to 9.7 million in 1987. While the number of whites below the poverty level increased from 17.5

million in 1970 to 21.6 million in 1981, in 1987 it decreased
to 21.4 million. However, the percentages of blacks and whites
living in poverty are more revealing. The percentage of blacks
with incomes below the poverty line increased from 1970 (33.5
percent) to 1981 (34.2 percent) and has oscillated slightly since
then (from 31.1 percent in 1986 to 33.1 percent in 1987). At
the same time, the poverty level for whites rose from 9.9 percent in 1970 to 14.1 percent in 1981 but fell back to 10.5 percent
in 1987 (Dewart, 1987).

Increases in black unemployment have significantly increased the number of blacks living in poverty. Unemployment
rates for black men and women have risen in almost all age
categories since 1965. These rates probably underestimate the
number of unemployed because they omit discouraged workers
who are no longer looking for jobs. Between 1972 and 1982 the
number of employed blacks increased by 19 percent nationally
(1.4 million). However, at the same time, the number of unemployed blacks increased by 1.2 million (from 900,000 in 1972
to 2.1 million in 1982). This represented an increase of 140 percent (Matney and Johnson, 1984).

According to the U.S. Bureau of Labor Statistics, the unemployment rate for blacks in 1972 and 1982 was twice that of
whites (10.3 percent for blacks versus 5 percent for whites in 1972;
18.9 percent for blacks versus 8.6 percent for whites in 1982).
In 1986, the spread between white and black unemployment
rates was even greater: 14.5 percent for blacks versus 6 percent
for whites. White teenagers between the ages of sixteen and nineteen averaged an unemployment rate of 20.4 percent in 1982,
while the unemployment rate for black teenagers was more than
twice as high (48 percent) during this time. In 1986 the spread
was also greater for this age group: whites aged sixteen to nineteen averaged an unemployment rate of 15.6 percent versus 39.3
percent for black teenagers.

Unemployment is directly related to educational attainment for both races. In 1982, whites and blacks with only high
school degrees were three times as likely to be unemployed as
college graduates; in 1986, high school graduates were two and
a half times as likely to be unemployed as those with college

degrees. But even when controlling for education, we find that a much higher percentage of blacks than whites are underemployed and unemployed (Darity, 1986; Smith, 1981). In 1982, 8.3 percent of black college graduates were unemployed versus 2.9 percent of white college graduates; in 1986, 5.3 percent of blacks with college degrees were unemployed versus 2.3 percent of whites with degrees.

Those blacks who are employed are heavily concentrated in the lower-paying, lower-status jobs within most occupations. In 1985, blacks in the U.S. civilian labor force were found primarily in three occupational sectors: technical, sales, and administration (26 percent); service (24 percent); and operators, fabricators, and laborers (23 percent) (Matney and Johnson, 1984). Only 14 percent of black workers were employed in the managerial and professional sector in 1985 versus 25 percent of white workers (U.S. Bureau of the Census, 1985).

Implications of Demographics and Enrollment Trends

Demographic trends indicate that blacks represent a younger and faster growing population than do whites. They will most likely be concentrated in the Sun Belt and near major metropolitan areas. Black children will be more likely to live in female-headed, single-parent families and will also be more likely to live in poverty. The educational system is already feeling the impact of these trends, and their effect will be even more pronounced in the coming decades. The present and projected educational and social status and needs of blacks thus present problems and challenges that are critical to the health and welfare of our nation's economy.

In the absence of adequate and prompt response to the problems and challenges described, the question of who will bear their brunt or be most affected by them becomes relevant. Obviously black students and their parents must rally to raise public awareness regarding these issues. But apart from these individuals, certain educational institutions that have traditionally dealt with minority populations will be the most likely source of solutions. These institutions include public elementary and secondary schools (especially those located in the nation's urban school districts), two-year and four-year public institutions, and the nation's predominantly black colleges.

Public Elementary and Secondary Schools. Between 1976 and 1984, the racial and ethnic composition of the nation's public schools changed considerably, with the number of white students declining and the number and proportion of minority students increasing (Stern, 1987). This was especially true for the twenty largest school districts in the United States. These school districts averaged a 70 percent minority enrollment (one out of every four minority students attended these schools versus one out of every twenty whites). Black students made up more than 16 percent of the total public elementary and secondary school enrollment in 1980. Analysts predict that the school population in at least five states will be more than 50 percent minority by 1990 (U.S. Department of Education, Center for Education Statistics, 1987).

It is unlikely that most underrepresented minorities in the future will have the opportunity to attend a good private or public school. Consequently, many of the students from these groups will continue to attend lower-quality inner-city public schools. Many of these schools already suffer from overcrowding and teacher shortages. Unless these schools are better supported, they may well become totally incapable of meeting the needs of the growing numbers of minority students.

Two-Year Institutions. Black enrollment in two-year institutions came largely as a result of the dramatic increase in the number of two-year colleges established between 1961 and 1976 (Mingle, 1981). These colleges created urban campuses and opened admissions to include more disadvantaged minorities. In 1980, 42 percent of black undergraduates were in two-year colleges; by 1988, this figure had grown slightly to 43 percent. The increase in minority enrollment in two-year colleges has been attributed primarily to rising costs and admissions standards at many white four-year colleges, along with a decrease in financial aid (Stern and Williams, 1987). It is predicted that both an increase in the costs and standards in white four-year colleges and an increase in the enrollment of blacks in two-year colleges will be prominent educational trends in the future (Blackwell, 1987). However, this has serious implications for degree attainment for blacks. Students at two-year institutions are more likely to drop out of college than are those at four-year institutions. Moreover, relatively few students make the transition from two-year to four-year institutions, and blacks have the lowest transfer rate of all racial/ethnic groups (Brown, 1987). Therefore two-year institutions will have to work more closely with four-year colleges and universities in order to open the educational pipeline for minority students.

Four-Year Institutions. Since 1980, there have been some fluctuations in the numbers of black undergraduates at four-year colleges and universities. Some predominantly white institutions have established linkages with inner-city junior high schools and high schools and have set special admissions criteria to identify and attract greater numbers of minority students. Despite the creation of these special support programs geared to meet the needs of minority students, however, four-year institutions have been far less successful at retaining and graduating students than attracting them. These programs have been faulted for not integrating black students into the student body. The number of black students on a given campus appears to make a difference. Richardson, Simmons, and de los Santos (1987) explain that when minority enrollments approach 20 percent of the total campus population, the campus environment changes from accommodation of minority students through special programs to incorporation of them into the mainstream of institutional culture.

Black Colleges. Traditionally, the nation's black colleges were the prime providers of higher education for black and low-income students. Black colleges experienced an increase in enrollments in the late 1960s and early 1970s as a result of expanded curricular offerings and significantly lower tuition than that charged by predominantly white colleges and universities.

Though enrollments of black undergraduates in black colleges decreased between 1980 (16.8 percent) and 1986 (16.3 percent), black colleges still awarded 34 percent of bachelor's degrees, a number that has remained fairly stable since 1981–82 (American Council on Education, 1987b). Black colleges may increase their enrollments in the future as a result of the present questioning of the relevancy of the *Adams* mandate and what appears to be a decline in commitment to federally mandated higher education desegregation ("Judge Dismisses the Case . . . ," 1988). Moreover, the perception of an increasingly unfriendly environment for black students on predominantly white campuses due to an increase in the number of racial incidents will make attendance at one of the black colleges a more attractive choice for blacks.

However, the current economic instability of many black colleges may render them unable to accommodate and adequately educate substantial numbers of black and low-income students in the future. Although the U.S. military may assume a larger role in the postsecondary career of black students, greater priority must be given to making sure that two-year colleges produce more transfer students and that four-year white colleges make adjustments to better accommodate black students so that they are able to graduate. Four-year white colleges must look to the black colleges as a model, for they have been the most successful at retaining and graduating black students despite the poor preparation of many of these students. At the same time, the state and federal governments must offer more attractive financial aid packages so that the choice of pursuing a higher education is a viable one for children from poor and disadvantaged families.

Meeting the Future Challenge

Serious challenges confront our nation. The first challenge involves taking a different view of underrepresented minorities. Specifically, this means viewing minorities as an investment rather than as a problem. In this regard, it is worth recalling that most U.S. minorities are products of the system. Many of these individuals came to the United States on an involuntary basis. More importantly, a substantial part of the U.S. economy and society have been, and continue to be, built on the "blood, sweat, and labor" of minority workers. The issue of the current declining status of underrepresented minorities and its implications for the future welfare of society must assume top priority on national and state agendas. It is critical that an adequate number of underrepresented minorities be systematically involved in the formulation and discussion of such agendas.

Since meeting the challenges of minority education will not be cost free, national and state governments must be prepared to commit adequate funds and resources toward this end. They must be prepared to improve the availability and kinds of financial assistance for black students. In 1981, nearly half of all black college-bound students came from families with incomes under $12,000. Financial aid is important not only as an incentive but also as a retention device. Black students are nearly twice as likely to stay in college if they receive aid (Darling-Hammond, 1985). Resources will also be needed to improve the quality and conditions of minority education, as well as the preparation of minority students. Increasing the job skills and job preparation of minority youth for more competitive employment will also be necessary. In this regard, national and state initiatives must be joined with the monetary support and active involvement of prospective employers from both the public and private sectors. In addition, two issues deserve special attention: improving the educational data base (the authors can testify to the difficulty of locating current and useful data) and responding to teacher shortages.

Improving the Data Base. To monitor and improve the progress of blacks and underrepresented minorities in higher education, there is a dire need for more and better detailed racial and ethnic data on the current educational status and future enrollment and degree attainment projections of minorities, and this information is needed on both the state and the national level. Some of these data are disaggregated by sex, but none are disaggregated by race. There is simply no way to develop effective educational policies for minorities if we cannot clearly identify or differentiate between or among these groups. Commonly found categories for reporting data on minorities such as minority versus nonminority or Hispanics versus blacks will not suffice. Similarly, the gross census categories for reporting age will be increasingly problematic for both research and policy purposes given the different projected growth rates among different minority age cohorts and the different policy implications for these age cohorts.

Most of the existing data and studies on minority education entail survey research on minority student achievement, attainment, and aspirations. By contrast, very few studies have focused on institutions as the primary unit of analysis. There is a pressing need for qualitative and institutionally based case-study research. This research should be geared primarily toward (1) describing what educational institutions are doing regarding minority education, (2) assessing the effects of these institutions on minority student outcomes, and (3) determining and describing the environmental conditions and context in which minority education takes place. Such data are critical to understanding and enhancing minority student achievement.

Projected Shortage of Public School Teachers. An increasingly important issue in the coming decade for educational practitioners and policymakers will be the decreasing supply of public school teachers. Current shortages in the number of students interested in becoming teachers will have a serious impact on our ability to develop an adequate number of teachers who will be willing and able to teach minority youth.

It is estimated that 23 percent of each college graduating class will be needed to meet the demand for teachers in the 1990s (Carnegie Task Force on Teaching, 1986). The current increase of about one-half of 1 percent annually in the college graduating class of teachers will not be adequate to meet this demand. Black teachers will be even scarcer in the future since the number and proportion of blacks and Hispanics who are pursuing majors in education are decreasing (Larke, 1988; Brown, 1987). The more talented members of these groups are choosing majors that promise better paying jobs. This has a negative effect on both the quality and quantity of the minority teaching pool. It also means that black students will have far fewer role models and mentors of their own race to help them achieve their educational goals.

In the absence of more attractive incentives, it will be difficult to recruit adequate numbers of majority teachers to teach low-income minority youth. Even those majority teachers who are willing to teach minority youth may not be able to do so effectively. Larke (1988) noted that, in addition to being creative and academically competent, teachers who instruct minority youth must be bilingual (in the case of Hispanics) and must have adequate experience with and understanding of minority culture and minority youth.

Competent, willing, and experienced majority and minority teachers will be needed in the future to meet the academic and personal needs of minority youth. Two types of teacher education programs are needed. The first should be designed to promote multicultural education and facilitate a greater understanding of minority cultures. A second set of programs should be designed to improve the success rate of minority teachers and minority prospective teachers on teacher certification examinations. Controversy and debate continue about these programs, but given the high rate of failure of minority teachers on these exams and the declining numbers of minority teachers, there doesn't seem to be any alternative.

Sounding the Alarm

A final step that must be taken by all committed individuals and organizations is to sound the alarm. The alarm must be sounded continuously regarding the significance and magnitude of the current issues and problems, as well as the future challenges, that surround minority education.

Minority parents must become more involved in the education of their youngsters. However, adequate awareness of the problems and issues must precede such involvement. Minority and majority communities, in general, need to become more informed about the current status of and future prospects for the education of minorities. Sponsoring national conferences on these issues, disseminating relevant publications, and involving the media are important methods for sounding the alarm, as is putting these issues at the forefront of major public and private organizational agendas. Forming alliances with state education agencies should also prove useful.

The 1990s will unquestionably provide a challenging opportunity to help turn the wheels of progress forward in the face of a decline in federal involvement and to search for national leadership and commitment regarding minority education. The extent and manner of the response by individuals and institutions to this challenge are decisive factors that remain to be determined in the future.

References

American Council on Education. *Fact Book on Minorities in Higher Education.* Washington, D.C.: American Council on Education, 1987a.

American Council on Education. *Minorities in Higher Education.* Sixth Annual Status Report. Washington, D.C.: American Council on Education, 1987b.

Blackwell, J. *Mainstreaming Outsiders: The Production of Black Professionals.* Bayside, N.Y.: General Hall, 1981.

Blackwell, J. "Race and Education: Issues Affecting Black and Hispanics in the Educational Pipeline." Paper presented at Conference on Race and Ethnic Relations, Texas A&M University, 1987.

Blake, E., Jr. "Equality for Blacks." *Change,* 1987, *19* (3), 10–13.

Brown, S. *Minorities in the Graduate Education Pipeline.* Princeton, N.J.: Educational Testing Service, 1987.

Carnegie Task Force on Teaching. *A Nation Prepared.* New York: Carnegie Commission, 1986.

College Board. *Equality and Excellence: The Educational Status of Black Americans.* New York: College Board, 1985.

Copeland, E. J. "Trends in Black Participation in Graduate Education: Barriers to Access, Possible Alternatives." Paper presented at 2nd National Conference on Issues Facing Black Administrators at Predominantly White Colleges and Universities, Cambridge, Mass., 1984.

Darity, W. A., Jr. "The Human Capital Approach to Black-White Earnings Inequality: Some Unsettled Questions." *Journal of Human Resources,* 1986, *17,* 90–98.

Darling-Hammond, L. *Equality and Excellence.* New York: College Board, 1985.

Dewart, J. *The State of Black America.* New York: National Urban League, 1987.

Fleming, J. E. "Blacks in Higher Education to 1954: A Historical Overview." In G. E. Thomas (ed.), *Black Students in Higher Education: Conditions and Experiences in the 1970s.* Westport, Conn.: Greenwood Press, 1981.

Gerald, D. E. "Public Elementary and Secondary Enrollments: Outlook to the Year 2000." *Bulletin-OERI,* Center for Education Statistics, Washington, D.C., 1987.

Horn, P. J. "Public School Teachers." Center for Education Statistics, Washington, D.C., 1987.

"Judge Dismisses the Case Used for Fifteen Years to Prod States, U.S. on Campus Segregation." *Chronicle of Higher Education,* Jan. 15, 1988.

Larke, P. "Minority Teachers—An Endangered Species." Paper presented at Conference on Race and Ethnic Relations, Texas A&M University, Feb. 1988.

Lenth, C. *Demography and Higher Education in the Changing Southwest: Texas.* Boulder, Colo.: Information Clearinghouse, Western Interstate Commission for Higher Education, 1987.

Malcom, S. M. "The Place of Minorities in the Scientific and Technical Work Force." *The Black Scholar,* Sept./Oct. 1985, pp. 51–53.

Matney, W. C., and Johnson, D. L. *America's Black Population: A Statistical View, 1970–1982.* Washington, D.C.: U.S. Department of Commerce, 1984.

Mingle, J. "The Opening of White Colleges and Universities to Black Students." In G. E. Thomas (ed.), *Black Students in Higher Education: Conditions and Experiences in the 1970s.* Westport, Conn.: Greenwood Press, 1981.

Mingle, J. *Focus on Minorities: Trends in Higher Education Participation and Success.* Denver, Colo.: Education Commission of the States and State Higher Education Executive Officers, 1987.

Murdock, S., and Hamm, R. "The Implications of Changing Demographics for Minority Enrollment in Higher Education." Paper presented at Texas A&M University System bi-monthly meeting of the chancellor and the presidents of the academic institutions at Texas A&M University, Galveston, 1987.

National Science Board Commission on Precollege Education in Mathematics, Science, and Technology. *Educating Americans for the 21st Century: A Plan for Improving Mathematics, Science, and Technology Education for all American Elementary and Secondary Students.* Washington, D.C.: National Science Foundation, 1984.

Nettles, M. *Financial Aid and Minority Participation in Graduate Education.* Princeton, N.J.: Educational Testing Service, 1987.

Orfield, G., and others. *The Chicago Study of Access and Choice in Higher Education.* Chicago: University of Chicago Committee on Public Policy Studies Research Project, 1984.

Peterson, M. W., and others. *Black Students on White Campuses: The Impacts of Increased Black Enrollments.* Ann Arbor, Mich.: Institute for Social Research, 1978.

Richardson, R. C., Jr., Simmons, H., and de los Santos, A. G., Jr. "Graduating Minority Students: Lessons from Ten Success Stories." *Change,* 1987, *19* (3), 20–27.

Sells, L. W. "The Mathematics Filter and the Education of Women and Minorities." Paper presented at the annual meeting of the American Association for the Advancement of Science, Boston, 1976.

Smith, D. J. *Unemployment and Racial Minorities.* London: Policy Studies Institute, 1981.

Spencer, G. *Projections of the Population of the United States by Age, Sex, and Race: 1983 to 2080.* Washington, D.C.: U.S. Bureau of the Census, 1984.

Stern, J. D., and Williams, M. F. (eds.). *The Condition of Education.* Washington, D.C.: Center for Education Statistics, 1987.

Swinton, D. "Economic Progress for Black Americans in the

Post Civil Rights Era." Paper presented at Conference on Race and Ethnic Relations, Texas A&M University, 1988.

Thomas, G. E. "Black Students in U.S. Graduate and Professional Schools in the 1980s: A National and Institutional Assessment." *Harvard Educational Review,* 1987, *57,* 261–282.

Tienda, M. "Race, Ethnicity, and the Politics of Inequality: Approaching the 1990s." *Sociological Spectrum,* 1989, *1* (9), 23–52.

U.S. Bureau of the Census. *What's It Worth? Educational Background and Economic Status: Spring 1984.* Current Population Reports, Series P–70, no. 11. Washington, D.C.: U.S. Government Printing Office, 1984.

U.S. Bureau of the Census. *Money, Income, and Poverty Status of Families and Persons in the United States.* Current Population Reports, Series P–60, no. 157. Washington, D.C.: U.S. Government Printing Office, 1985.

U.S. Department of Education, Center for Education Statistics, Survey Report. "Trends in Minority Enrollment in Higher Education, Fall 1976 to Fall 1986." Washington, D.C.: U.S. Government Printing Office, 1988.

U.S. Department of Education, Center for Education Statistics. "Public and Private Elementary and Secondary Enrollment: Outlook to the Year 2000." Washington, D.C.: U.S. Government Printing Office, 1987.

Western Interstate Commission for Higher Education. *Shaping the Future of the Southwest: Background Materials on Minorities in Education and the Economy of the Southwest.* Boulder, Colo.: Western Interstate Commission for Higher Education, 1987.

Western Interstate Commission for Higher Education and the College Board. *Minorities in Higher Education: The Changing Southwest.* Boulder, Colo.: Western Interstate Commission for Higher Education, 1984.

Young, A. M. "One-Fourth of Adult Labor Force Are College Graduates." *Monthly Labor Review,* Feb. 1985, p. 43.

E/o Chap. 4

p 87+88 (DIT)

chap.

5

Asians

by Bob H. Suzuki (SP)

For most of their history in the United States, Asian Americans have been so few in number that they have tended to be viewed as a relatively insignificant minority group. During the past decade, however, they have emerged as the nation's fastest growing minority (Bouvier and Agresta, 1985) and are now seen by many as a minority group that will play an increasingly influential role in American society and that therefore deserves much more attention than it has been given in the past.

This chapter describes the changing demographics of Asian Americans and the implications of these changes for higher education. It adopts the definition of Asian Americans formulated by Gardner, Robey, and Smith (1985): Asian Americans are immigrants, refugees, and the U.S.-born descendants of immigrants from Asia, including Pakistan and the countries lying east of it in South Asia, Southeast Asia, and East Asia but not in Soviet Asia or the Pacific Islands. To the extent possible, Asians will be treated separately from Pacific Islanders, except when the only data available are aggregated data for both groups. The six largest Asian groups on which this chapter focuses are Chinese, Filipinos, Japanese, Asian Indians, Koreans, and Vietnamese.

Current Demographic Data on Asian Americans

This section presents current demographic data on Asian Americans, including data on immigration, population, and socioeconomic and educational characteristics.

Recent Immigration. Asian immigration has grown at an explosive rate during the the past two decades. Since 1965, for example, the immigration rate from Asia increased by six to eight times. This rate has averaged around 250,000 to 275,000 immigrants per year over the five-year period 1981 to 1985 and has exceeded that from any other region of the world (Immigration and Naturalization Service, 1986).

The enormous increase in Asian immigration was the direct result of the changes made in U.S. immigration laws in 1965. However, while these statutory changes finally opened the doors to Asian immigration, the driving forces behind this immigration have been the social, political, and economic conditions in such countries as South Korea, Hong Kong, and the Philippines. In addition, the outflow of refugees from Indochina following the end of the Vietnam War added greatly to the number of Asians now living in the United States. The predominance of Asian immigration should come as no surprise if one considers that nearly 60 percent of the world's population lives in Asia (U.S. Bureau of the Census, 1986). If U.S. immigration laws had not discriminated against Asian immigrants, the total immigration from Asia might have exceeded that from any other region of the world, and the Asian-American population might constitute the majority of the U.S. population today.

Population. No minority group in America is experiencing a larger percentage increase in population than Asian Americans. As shown in Table 5.1, the Asian population increased between 116 and 143 percent during the 1970s. This rate of growth was about twenty times greater than that of the white population, more than ten times greater than that of the general population, and almost double that of the next fastest growing minority group. p.89 - Table 5.1

A breakdown of the Asian population into the six largest ethnic groups for 1970 and 1980, as well as estimates of the populations of these groups for 1985, is presented in Table 5.2. The 1985 estimates, by Gardner, Robey, and Smith (1985), show that the total Asian population of over 5 million had increased by nearly 50 percent since 1980. As of September 30, 1985, Asians constituted 2.1 percent of the total U.S. population.

IS CAPT

Table 5.1. U.S. Population by Race/Ethnicity, 1970 and 1980. (sources)

(6)

Race/Ethnicity	1970		1980		% Increase, 1970 to 1980
	Number	%	Number	%	
White	168,454,466	82.9	180,602,838	79.8	7.2
Black	22,580,289	11.1	26,091,857	11.5	15.6
Hispanic	9,294,509	4.6	14,326,268	6.3	54.1
Asian	**1,426,148**	**0.7**	**3,466,421**	**1.5**	**143.1**[a] note a
Pacific Islander	100,179	-	259,566	0.1	N.A.[b] note b
Native American	817,268	0.4	1,478,523	0.7	78.7
Other	516,673	0.3	--	-	
Total	203,199,532	100.0	226,225,473	100.0	11.3 R/T

NOTE [a]Asian Indians were not included in 1970 but were included in 1980. The increase, excluding Asian Indians, was 116 percent. R/ Table
NOTE [b]Since only Hawaiians were included in 1970, calculation of this increase would have no meaning. R/ Table
Sources: U.S. Bureau of the Census, 1981, 1983b.

As Table 5.2 shows, in 1985 the Chinese and Filipino populations each exceeded one million persons. The Japanese, who made up 41 percent of the total Asian population in 1970, represented less than 15 percent of that population in 1985. Particularly startling is the rapid growth of the next three largest groups — Asian Indians, Koreans, and Vietnamese, each of whose populations exceeded 500,000 in 1985. Table 5.2 also indicates that foreign-born Asians made up nearly 60 percent of the total Asian population in the United States, ranging from a high of 90.5 percent for the Vietnamese to a low of 28.4 percent for the Japanese. p.90 Table 5.2

Although the Asian population was somewhat more dispersed geographically in 1980 than in 1970, it continues to be concentrated in the thirteen states (including Alaska and Hawaii) defined as the West by the U.S. Bureau of the Census (1983b). Whereas 70 percent of the Asian population lived in the West in 1970, only 56 percent lived there in 1980.

p.91 *Socioeconomic Characteristics.* Table 5.3 compares the median family incomes in 1979 of whites, blacks, and Hispanics against those of the six largest Asian groups. The median

IS CAPT

(9)

Table 5.2 Asian American Population, 1970, 1980, and 1985. (sauteen)

Ethnic Group	1970		1980			1985		% Increase, 1980–1985
	Number	%	Number	%	% Foreign Born	Number	%	
Total	1,426,148	100.0	3,466,421	100.0	58.6	5,147,900	100.0	48.5
Chinese	431,583	30.3	812,178	23.4	63.3	1,079,400	21.0	32.9
Filipino	336,583	23.6	781,894	22.6	66.3	1,051,600	20.4	34.5
Japanese	588,324	41.3	716,331	20.7	28.4	766,300	14.9	7.0
Asian Indian	N.A.ᵃ	-	387,223	11.2	70.4	525,600	10.2	35.7
Korean	69,510	4.9	357,393	10.3	81.8	542,400	10.5	51.8
Vietnamese	N.A.	-	245,025	7.1	90.5	634,200	12.3	158.8
Other Asians	N.A.	-	166,377	4.8	--	548,400	10.7	229.6

NOTE ᵃAsian Indians were classified as white until the 1980 census. R/Table

Sources: U.S. Bureau of the Census, 1983a; Gardner, Robey, and Smith, 1985.

R/T

Table 5.3. Median Income and Poverty Level by Race/Ethnicity, 1979.

Race/Ethnicity	Median Family Income	Median Income of Full-Time Worker	% of Families Below Poverty Level
White	$20,835	$15,572	7.0
Black	12,598	11,327	26.5
Hispanic	14,712	11,650	21.3
Chinese	22,559	15,753	10.5
Filipino	23,687	13,690	6.2
Japanese	27,354	16,829	4.2
Korean	20,459	14,224	13.1
Asian Indian	24,993	18,707	7.4
Vietnamese	12,840	11,641	35.1

Sources: U.S. Bureau of the Census, 1983a; Gardner, Robey, and Smith, 1985.

incomes of Japanese, Chinese, Filipino, Korean, and Asian Indian families were all above those of white families and considerably above those of black and Hispanic families. Only the median income of Vietnamese families was substantially below that of white families and, for that matter, also below that of Hispanic families. The median income of full-time workers was above that of whites for the Japanese, Chinese, and Asian Indians; only that of the Vietnamese was substantially below that of whites and about equal to that of blacks and Hispanics. For the Japanese, Filipinos, and Asian Indians, the proportion of families living below the poverty level was comparable to that of white families, whereas considerably more Chinese, Korean, and Vietnamese families were living below the poverty level than were white families. TABLE 5.3

These statistics on the incomes of Asian Americans indicate that most of them are doing remarkably well economically. Even the Vietnamese, most of whom arrived in the United States only a few years before the 1980 census, appear to be making rapid progress and undoubtedly are much better off today than they were in 1980. However, these statistics by themselves are somewhat misleading; I will analyze them in more detail later in this chapter to give a more accurate picture of the socioeconomic status of Asian Americans.

IS CAPT

Table 5.4. Age Distribution and Median Age by Race/Ethnicity, 1980 (source

| Race/ | % | | | | | Median |
Ethnicity	Under 5	5–19	20–44	45–64	Over 64	Age
Total	7.2	24.8	37.1	19.7	11.3	30.0
White	6.7	23.6	36.9	20.6	12.1	31.3
Black	9.1	30.8	36.5	15.8	7.8	24.9
Hispanic	11.3	31.8	39.0	13.4	4.6	23.2
AI/Alaskan[a]	10.1	32.6	38.6	13.4	5.2	24.0
Chinese	7.1	22.2	45.7	18.1	6.9	29.6
Filipino	9.0	26.2	44.1	13.5	7.2	28.5
Japanese	5.3	18.9	41.5	27.0	7.3	33.5
Korean	10.6	29.3	47.2	10.5	2.4	26.0
Asian Indian	11.1	21.0	49.9	10.1	8.0	30.1
Vietnamese	10.0	36.5	43.6	8.0	1.9	21.5
Asian/PI[b]	8.6	24.9	44.8	15.7	5.9	28.4

NOTE [a]AI/Alaskan = American Indian/Alaskan Native.

NOTE [b]Asian/PI = Asian/Pacific Islander population. Since Pacific Islanders were only a small proportion (about 7.5 percent) of the Asian population, these figures should be a good estimate for Asians alone.

Source: U.S. Bureau of the Census, 1983a.

Table 5.4 describes the age distribution of Asian Americans. Except for the Japanese, whose median age (33.5) is considerably higher than that of the general population (30), the Asian American population is a relatively young one compared to the white population but older than the black and Hispanic populations. The percentage of Asians under five years of age is higher than that of whites, especially in the case of Koreans, Asian Indians, and Vietnamese. Asians and whites have approximately the same proportion of their populations aged five to nineteen. However, there are considerably more Asians than whites aged twenty to forty-four and considerably fewer aged forty-five and over. Table 5.4

Educational Characteristics. Data compiled in the 1980 census (U.S. Bureau of the Census, 1983a) show that all the Asian groups had a consistently higher rate of enrollment in educational institutions at practically all ages than other racial/

ethnic groups, including whites. Even at the preschool level, ages three to four, the percentage of Asian children enrolled in school was considerably higher than that of white children (40 percent versus 32 percent), suggesting that Asian parents may place greater emphasis on education from the time their children are very young. At the other end of the age range, college-age Asians (eighteen to thirty-four) were also enrolled in institutions of higher education at a significantly higher rate than were other groups.

The emphasis placed on education by Asians is also reflected in Table 5.5, which displays data from the 1980 census on the percentages of persons twenty-five years or older who were high school graduates and who completed four or more years of college. Almost 80 percent of Asian males and over 70 percent of Asian females were high school graduates in 1980, percentages that were higher than those for their white counterparts and considerably higher than those of other minority groups. At the higher education level, nearly 40 percent of Asian males and 27 percent of Asian females had completed four or

IS CAPT.

**Table 5.5. Schooling Completed,
by Sex and Race/Ethnicity, for Persons 25 Years or Older, 1980.** (sources)

Race/Ethnicity	% High School Graduates		% Completed 4 + Years College	
	Male	Female	Male	Female
White	69.6	68.1	21.3	13.3
Black	50.8	51.5	8.4	8.3
Hispanic	45.4	42.7	9.4	6.0
AI/Alaskan[a]	57.0	54.1	9.2	6.3
Asian/PI[b]	78.8	71.4	39.8	27.0
Chinese	75.2	67.4	43.8	29.5
Filipino	73.1	67.4	32.2	29.5
Japanese	84.2	79.5	35.2	19.7
Korean	90.0	70.6	52.4	22.0
Asian Indian	88.8	71.5	68.5	35.5
Vietnamese	71.3	53.6	18.2	7.9

[a]AI/Alaskan = American Indian/Alaskan Native.
[b]Asian/PI = Asian/Pacific Islander.
Sources: U.S. Bureau of the Census, 1983a, 1984.

(Half page)

more years of college, about twice the rate of their white counterparts. Table 5.5

pp 94+95   Although enrollments in the public schools (kindergarten through twelfth grade) have been declining nationally since 1970, the enrollments of Asian students have increased from 535,000 (1.2 percent) in 1976 to 994,000 (2.5 percent) in 1984, an increase of 85.8 percent. Over the same period, the number of Hispanic students increased by 28.2 percent, whereas the numbers of white, black, and American Indian/Alaskan Native students decreased (Stern and Williams, 1987).

Enrollments in higher education have been steadily increasing for several decades. As Table 5.6 shows, between 1976 and 1986, the combined enrollments at two- and four-year institutions increased from 10,986,000 to 12,502,000, an increase of 13.8 percent. During the same ten-year period, Asian enrollments increased 198,000 to 448,000, an increase of 126 percent. Correspondingly, Asian students increased as a proportion of the total student population from 1.8 percent in 1976 to 3.6 percent in 1986. During the same period, the proportion of white students declined from 82.6 percent to 79.3 percent.

It is also interesting to note that the number of nonresident alien students increased from 219,000 students in 1976 to 344,000 students in 1986, an increase of 57 percent. Between 1980–81 and 1985–86, the proportion of these foreign students who came from Asian countries increased from 30 percent to over 45 percent (Snyder, 1987). Therefore, of the 344,000 foreign students counted in 1986, approximately 150,000 were probably Asian students. Table 5.6

According to a 1984 survey of the Center for Education Statistics (Snyder, 1987), there were 382,000 Asian American students enrolled in institutions of higher education in the United States. Of these, 83 percent were enrolled in public institutions and 17 percent in private institutions. For white students, the comparable figures were 77 percent and 23 percent, respectively. Approximately 70 percent (301,000) of the Asian American students were undergraduates, of whom 47 percent were women, whereas 78 percent of the white students were undergraduates, of whom 52 percent were women. Graduate students represented

IS CAPT .

Table 5.6. Enrollment Trends in Higher Education,
Fall 1976 to Fall 1986 (in Thousands). (source)

Race/Ethnicity and Citizenship	Number Enrolled					
	1976	1978	1980	1982	1984	1986
Four-Year Institutions						
All Students	7,108	7,203	7,566	7,649	7,707	7,826
White	5,999	6,027	6,275	6,306	6,301	6,340
(%)	(84.4)	(83.7)	(82.9)	(82.4)	(81.9)	(81.0)
Asian/Pacific Islander	**119**	**138**	**162**	**193**	**223**	**262**
(%)	**(1.7)**	**(1.9)**	**(2.1)**	**(2.5)**	**(2.8)**	**(3.3)**
Nonresident Alien	177	201	241	270	282	291
(%)	(2.5)	(2.8)	(3.2)	(3.5)	(3.7)	(3.7)
Two-Year Institutions						
All Students	3,878	4,029	4,520	4,470	4,528	4,676
White	3,077	3,167	3,558	3,692	3,514	3,575
(%)	(79.3)	(78.6)	(78.7)	(77.9)	(77.6)	(76.5)
Asian/Pacific Islander	**79**	**97**	**124**	**158**	**167**	**186**
(%)	**(2.0)**	**(2.4)**	**(2.7)**	**(3.3)**	**(3.7)**	**(4.0)**
Nonresident Alien	42	52	64	61	53	53
(%)	(1.1)	(1.3)	(1.4)	(1.3)	(1.2)	(1.1)
All Institutions						
All Students	10,986	11,232	12,086	12,389	12,235	12,502
White	9,076	9,194	9,833	9,998	9,815	9,915
(%)	(82.6)	(81.9)	(81.4)	(80.7)	(80.2)	(79.3)
Asian/Pacific Islander	**198**	**235**	**286**	**351**	**390**	**448**
(%)	**(1.8)**	**(2.1)**	**(2.4)**	**(2.8)**	**(3.2)**	**(3.6)**
Nonresident Alien	219	253	305	331	335	344
(%)	(2.0)	(2.3)	(2.5)	(2.7)	(2.7)	(2.8)

Source: Evangelauf, 1988.

7.5 percent, or 28,500 (of whom 37 percent were women), of all Asian American college students, whereas 9 percent of the white students (of whom 48 percent were women) were at the graduate level. In addition, there were 9,200 Asian American students (2.4 percent) pursuing their first professional degrees and 42,800 Asian American students (11.1 percent) who were unclassified.

The major fields of study for the bachelor's degree pursued by Asian American students in 1980–81 are listed in Table 5.7. The most popular field of study for both Asian students

IS CAPT

Table 5.7. Bachelor's Degrees, by Field,
Earned by Asian/Pacific Islanders, 1980–81. (source)

| | All Groups | | Asian/PI | |
Major Field of Study	Number	(%)	Number	(%)
ALL FIELDS	934,800	100.0	18,794	100.0
Agriculture/Natural Resources	21,886	2.3	312	1.7
Architecture/Environmental Design	9,455	1.0	296	1.6
Biological Sciences	43,216	4.6	1,489	7.9
Business/Management	200,857	21.5	3,943	21.0
Communications	31,282	3.3	368	2.0
Computer/Information Sciences	15,120	1.6	669	3.6
Education	108,265	11.6	723	3.8
Engineering	74,954	8.0	3,066	16.3
Fine and Applied Arts	40,241	4.3	788	4.2
Health Professions	63,649	6.8	1,312	7.0
Law	776	0.1	5	-
Letters	40,028	4.3	460	2.4
Mathematics	11,078	1.2	391	2.1
Physical Sciences	23,950	2.6	596	3.2
Psychology	40,833	4.4	839	4.5
Social Sciences	100,647	10.8	1,645	8.8
Theology	5,807	0.6	58	0.3

Source: Vetter and Babco, 1984.

and students in general was business/management. About one-fifth of the Asian students and students in general earned bachelor's degrees in this field of study. The next most popular field of study for Asian students was engineering. Over 16 percent of the Asian students earned degrees in this field of study, compared with 8 percent of students in general. Education, the second most popular field of study for students in general, was pursued by nearly 12 percent of all students; however, less than 4 percent of the Asian students pursued this field. In fact, paradoxically, given their strong emphasis on education, Asians are quite underrepresented in the teaching profession, making up less than 1 percent of all elementary and secondary school teachers in 1980 (Vetter and Babco, 1984). Table 5.7.

The third most popular field of study for both Asian students and students in general was social sciences, which were pursued by 8.8 percent of the Asian students and 10.8 percent of all students. The fourth and fifth most popular fields of study for Asian students were the biological sciences and the health professions, respectively. A higher proportion of Asian students than students in general pursued degrees in the biological sciences, computer/information sciences, and mathematics, while a lower proportion pursued degrees in letters and education. The proportions of Asian students and students in general pursuing other fields of study were not significantly different.

While these data partially uphold the popular view that Asians tend to major in science- and math-based fields and to shun the fields that require verbal and linguistic skills, such as the humanities, they also indicate that Asians pursue a far more diverse range of majors than generally thought. For example, the proportions of Asian students pursuing degrees in the fine and applied arts, psychology, and the social sciences are comparable to those of all students, a finding that may be somewhat surprising to many.

In 1981, 3.1 percent of the faculty and 1 percent of the administrators in institutions of higher education were Asians (Wilson and Melendez, 1985). It would appear that Asians were adequately represented, if not overrepresented, among the faculty in higher education. In contrast, they appear to have been underrepresented among higher education administrators.

However, it should be noted that a 1979 survey of doctorate recipients (Maxfield, 1981) revealed that of the 8,615 academically employed Asian doctorates in the sciences and engineering, 90 percent were foreign-born. Even in the humanities, which do not attract nearly as many Asian foreign students because of the stronger English language skills needed in these fields, 81 percent of the 562 academically employed Asian doctorates were foreign-born. The high proportion of foreign-born Asian doctorates is not too surprising in view of the fact that many of them came from the higher socieconomic classes and represented the intellectual elite (perhaps the top 0.1 percent) of their countries of origin and were therefore likely to do well even as immigrants.

Based on the statistics presented above, it can be inferred that only about 10 percent, or about 1,400, of the 14,381 Asian faculty in higher education were born in the United States. The U.S.-born Asian faculty, therefore, represented only about 0.3 percent of all faculty in higher education. Since native-born Asians made up about 0.62 percent of the total U.S. population in 1980, U.S.-born Asian faculty were clearly underrepresented in higher education. This fact may have affirmative action implications, particularly since native-born Asians have borne the historical legacy of some 140 years of racial discrimination.

Model Minority Image

Given the glowing socioeconomic and educational characteristics of Asian Americans presented in the preceding sections, it is not surprising they have been labeled the "model minority" not only by the popular press but by academic scholars as well ("Success Story . . . ," 1971; "Japanese-U.S. Outdo Horatio Alger," 1977; "The New Whiz Kids," 1987; Oxnam, 1986; Peterson, 1978; Boodman, 1978). Actually, this stereotype is not new; it originated in the popular press of the mid 1960s when the supposed "success" of Asian Americans was still highly problematic ("Success Story of One Minority Group in U.S.," 1966; Peterson, 1966).

Many Asian Americans took strong exception to this overly felicitous view of their status and did not find it fortuitous that their success stories were being publicized at a time when the country was facing racial problems of major proportions (Uyematsu, 1971). Nevertheless, when the results of the 1970 census were published and showed impressive gains in the income and educational levels of Asian Americans, the model minority image was strongly reinforced and Asian Americans were extolled even more by the popular press.

Around this same time, however, a number of Asian American scholars began to delve more deeply into the subject (Sung, 1975; Cabezas, 1977; Suzuki, 1977; Chun, 1980). These scholars analyzed the 1970 census data more closely and critically and reached the conclusion that characterization of Asian Americans as a model minority was inaccurate, misleading, and a gross overgeneralization. They noted that while many Asian

Americans had, indeed, achieved middle-class status, there was still a far larger proportion of people with incomes below the poverty level among Asian Americans than among whites. They also found that even for the more educated, middle-class Asian Americans, the model minority stereotype remained quite problematic. Although the median incomes of Asian American families were higher than those of white families, the median incomes of individuals were found to be lower for Asian Americans than for whites. This apparent paradox was due to the following factors: (1) There was a larger proportion of Asian American families in which both spouses worked than among white families; (2) Asian American children remained with their families longer and thereby contributed longer to family income; and (3) Asian American families were larger on the average and therefore had more earners contributing to family income.

Furthermore, when income figures for Asian Americans were adjusted for such demographic variables as education, age, geographic location, and weeks worked per year, it was found that they were earning considerably less than their white counterparts. On the basis of such analyses, it appeared that Asian Americans were typically underemployed in lower-level positions that were not commensurate with their levels of education, age, and experience. Although Asian Americans had invested heavily in education, this did not appear to result in nearly as much earning power for them as it did for whites. This disparity was largely attributed to the persistence of racial discrimination.

It now appears, however, from the 1980 census data on incomes (Table 5.3) that Asian Americans have not only reached parity with whites but may have surpassed them. For the four largest Asian groups — Chinese, Filipinos, Japanese, and Asian Indians, who represent about three-quarters of the total Asian population — both median family and median individual incomes considerably exceed (with the singular exception of Korean individual income) those of their white counterparts.

Again, however, these gross statistics are misleading. Table 5.8 compares, by race and ethnicity, the income in 1979 of males in three age cohorts with similar levels of education. This comparison removes income differentials that may be due

IS CAPT

Table 5.8. Income in 1979 of Males 25 to 64 Years of Age
by Years of Schooling Completed and Race/Ethnicity (in Dollars). *(source)*

Race/Ethnicity	Age Cohort			
	25–34	35–44	45–54	55–64
White				
4 Years High School	14,484	18,259	19,371	16,711
4 Years College	16,706	25,574	28,399	26,686
Black				
4 Years High School	10,224	13,359	13,687	11,541
4 Years College	13,770	18,144	18,089	15,541
Hispanic				
4 Years High School	11,910	15,195	15,561	13,165
4 Years College	14,668	20,226	20,762	17,543
AI/Alaskan*				
4 Years High School	10,614	14,349	15,318	12,125
4 Years College	13,825	19,182	19,381	17,207
Asian/PI*				
4 Years High School	**10,950**	**14,682**	**16,829**	**15,642**
4 Years College	**14,661**	**18,801**	**20,863**	**13,760**

NOTE *AI/Alaskan = American Indian/Alaskan Native.
NOTE *Asian/PI = Asian/Pacific Islander.
Source: U.S. Bureau of the Census, 1984.

to age and years of schooling by holding these variables constant. As Table 5.8 shows, this kind of comparison reveals major income differentials between Asian and white males for all four age cohorts and at both levels of education. In fact, in a number of cases, the incomes of Asian males were substantially below even those of Hispanic males. Unfortunately, published Bureau of the Census tabulations provide these data only in aggregated form, not for specific Asian groups. Table 5.8

However, the U.S. Commission on Civil Rights (1986) has published disaggregated income data on Asian Americans based on the 1980 census. These data, which are presented in Table 5.9, show that the mean incomes of Japanese males with less than sixteen years of schooling have reached parity with those of whites, while the mean income of Japanese males with at least a college education is still somewhat below that of their white counterparts. However, the mean incomes of other Asian males are substantially below those of their white counterparts. For

example, in the case of males with less than eight years of schooling, the Chinese mean incomes are only 68 percent of whites';
with four years of college or more, their mean incomes are 85
percent of whites'. In contrast, Asian females generally do as
well as or better than their white counterparts for all levels of
education. However, they earn considerably less than their male
counterparts. Table 5.9 shows the major differences that are
revealed between the various Asian groups when the data are
disaggregated.

IS CAPT·

Table 5.9. Mean Annual Incomes for Prime Workers
(Ages 25 to 54) by Years of Schooling, Race/Ethnicity, and Sex, 1979. (source)

Years of Schooling	Japanese	Chinese	Filipino	Korean	Vietnamese	White
Male						
0–7	--[a]	$ 8,845	$10,448	--[a]	$ 8,405	$13,063
8–11	$15,866	11,693	12,505	$13,683	9,140	15,309
12–15	18,562	14,530	13,523	13,849	10,724	18,133
16 +	25,233	22,084	22,407	22,965	15,291	26,038
Female						
0–7	--[a]	$ 6,055	$ 7,040	$ 6,604	$ 5,686	$ 6,244
8–11	$ 7,805	6,516	7,101	6,181	6,822	6,476
12–15	9,468	9,125	9,043	7,690	6,893	8,049
16 +	13,114	12,630	14,052	12,099	12,546	11,341

NOTE [a]Fewer than 100 cases. R/Table
Source: U.S. Commission on Civil Rights, 1986.

In sum, the data strongly suggest that Asian Americans
continue to face inequities in income and employment. Although
many Asian Americans are well educated, have become professionals, and gain relatively easy access to entry-level jobs, they
appear to encounter subtle discrimination when they attempt
to move up in the occupational hierarchy to managerial, administrative, or executive positions (Yu, 1985). All this certainly
does not negate the extraordinary achievements of Asian Americans in education. But it does raise the two questions of why
Asian Americans continue to invest so heavily in education in
the face of perceived employment discrimination and why they
have been so successful in education.

While a comprehensive analysis of these questions is beyond the scope of this chapter, Tsang and Wing (1985) have suggested one reasonable and plausible explanation that could serve as a working hypothesis for future studies. They posit that because early Asian immigrants encountered so many discriminatory barriers to employment, these immigrants became especially sensitive to sectors in the labor market where job opportunities might be available to them. During and following World War II, there was an enormous expansion in war-related industries and government bureaucracies, creating job opportunities in the technological and bureaucratic sectors of the economy. Tsang and Wing (1985) note that "perhaps because hiring appeared to be based on merit, Asian Americans began to enter these professional and technical occupations. In order to qualify for these types of jobs, they invested in college. They faced few financial barriers in doing so; most Asian Americans lived then (and now) on the West Coast, where an excellent postsecondary educational system is publicly financed" (p. 32).

Tsang and Wing explain the educational success of Asian Americans in terms of the time they spend on learning in comparison with other groups. Their willingness to invest this time may be due both to their cultural backgrounds, which place great emphasis on education, and to their awareness of employment barriers and opportunities. Therefore, while the educational achievements of Asian Americans have been quite remarkable, these achievements may, ironically enough, be related to the continuing discriminatory barriers that they face in the job market. From that perspective, the celebration of Asian Americans as the model minority would appear to be premature at best and, at worst, a troubling deception.

Demographic Projections

This section makes projections about Asian immigration, population, and higher education enrollments.

Immigration Projections. By examining recent trends in Asian immigration, it seems reasonable to make one of two estimates: (1) that Asian immigration will level off at around 250,000 to 300,000 immigrants per year or (2) that Asian immigration will gradually increase by 10,000 to 12,000 immigrants per year above its current level (Arnold, Minocha, and Fawcett, 1987).

Even when using the more conservative figures, we can still estimate that between 1.25 and 1.5 million Asian immigrants entered this country between 1985 and 1990 and that an additional 2.5 to 3 million will follow in the 1990s.

Population Projections. Projections of the Asian population in the United States have been made by Gardner, Robey, and Smith (1985). According to their estimates, the Asian population will increase to 6.5 million by 1990 and to almost 10 million by the year 2000, nearly tripling the 1980 Asian population of just under 3.5 million. They estimate that, by the year 2000, Asians will make up almost 4 percent of the total U.S. population (projected to grow to 268 million). At least by 1990, and probably before, Filipinos will become the largest Asian group, growing to over 2 million in the year 2000. While the Chinese will remain the second largest group, with 1.6 million projected for the year 2000, three groups—the Vietnamese, Koreans, and Asian Indians—will pass the Japanese, who will become the sixth largest group by the end of the 1990s. These three groups will each have populations exceeding one million in the year 2000.

Geographically, Asians will probably continue to be concentrated in the West, but to a lesser degree than they are now. There should be a greater dispersion of Asians to other parts of the country over the next two decades, as the immigrants and their offspring adjust to and integrate into the larger society.

Higher Education Enrollment Projections. The data on higher education enrollment trends previously presented in Table 5.6 showed the dramatic increase (126 percent) in the total enrollment of Asian students and the leveling off of the enrollment of white students over the past decade. A linear projection of the Asian population data indicates a very steep rate of increase — approximately 30,000 students per year. If one assumes that Asian enrollments will continue to increase at this rate from 1986 to 1990 and that white and total enrollments will remain level over the same period, there would be 570,000 Asian students enrolled in higher education by 1990, constituting 4.5 percent of all students. If the same assumptions are made to project enrollments for the 1990s, Asian enrollments could climb to 870,000, or 7 percent of all students.

These projected increases in Asian enrollments are likely to have a relatively uniform impact on all sectors of higher education. From 1976 to 1986, about 55 to 60 percent of all Asian students were enrolled in four-year institutions, and the remaining 40 to 45 percent of these students attended two-year institutions (Snyder, 1987). There are no clear-cut trends in these data to indicate that these proportions will change significantly in the future. Therefore, both types of institutions are likely to experience similar increases in Asian enrollments over the next several years.

From 1976 to 1986, the proportion of all Asian students who attended private institutions increased very slightly, but steadily, from 16.2 to 16.9 percent (Snyder, 1987). While this slight increase may not be indicative of a significant trend, it undoubtedly has some relationship to the improvement in the socioeconomic status of Asian Americans during this period. Since their status is likely to continue to improve, a slightly larger proportion of Asian students may be expected to attend private institutions in the future. However, the impact of such a slight shift of Asian students from public to private institutions will probably be barely discernible.

In states such as California, New York, Hawaii, and Illinois, where the largest numbers of Asian students attend college, they are likely to represent an even more substantial proportion of the total student population over the next decade. On some campuses in California, this proportion of Asian students may be as high as 30 to 40 percent. Obviously, these projections have important implications for institutions of higher education.

Forces for Change

There are a number of societal forces at work both in our nation and throughout the world that may strongly influence future changes in the demographics of Asian Americans and may have a major impact on our institutions of higher education. Two of these forces will be briefly described in this section.

Pacific Rim Era. In 1982, for the first time in history, U.S. trade with the Pacific Rim nations exceeded that with the European nations. This trade is expected to grow at a very fast rate over the next several decades — a period now often referred to as the Pacific Rim Era. Concomitant with this increase in trade has been a sharp rise in the influx of immigrants from Pacific Rim countries into the United States, especially immigrants from Asia and Latin America.

Because of the huge influx of capital from the Pacific Rim trade, economic analysts expect the financial center of the country to shift eventually from New York City to Los Angeles, perhaps within the next few decades. And since cultural infusion usually follows closely on the heels of capital infusion, the various Pacific Rim cultures, particularly those of Asia, may be expected to influence and transform American culture to a greater and greater degree (Lockwood and Leinberger, 1987). In addition to this cultural transformation, we can also expect the United States to be transformed economically, politically, and socially by these changing influences. As our commercial, cultural, and political interactions with the Pacific Rim nations increase, our knowledge (or lack thereof) of the histories, cultures, politics, economies, and languages of these nations will become increasingly relevant to the present and future well-being and viability of our nation.

In view of the global changes described above, it is essential that international perspectives be incorporated in the college curriculum. If present and future generations of college students are to be adequately prepared to meet the challenges that lie ahead of them, they must acquire far more knowledge of non-Western nations than most of them can currently acquire through existing academic programs.

Immigration. A number of Asian countries are undergoing social and political changes that could significantly affect the rates at which they send emigrants to the United States. On the one hand, repressive political regimes in South Korea and the Philippines, which were partly responsible for the high emigrant outflows from these countries, have yielded to democratic governments. With greater freedom and improved economic conditions in these countries, their emigration rates may decline. On the other hand, emigration from Hong Kong can be expected to remain high at least until 1997, when control over this longtime British colony will revert to the People's Republic of China. Future levels of emigration from Hong Kong will depend on the policies instituted by the Chinese government. The relationship between Taiwan and the People's Republic of China also remains uncertain and will surely affect future emigration rates from Taiwan. China itself appears to be moving toward an "open-door" policy that could measurably increase emigration from its vast population (Arnold, Minocha, and Fawcett, 1987).

The large flow of Indochinese refugees into the United States is expected to continue for several more years. As of 1984, it was estimated that 350,000 Indochinese remained in refugee camps along the Thai border. Increasing numbers of Vietnamese immigrants are also entering this country through the Orderly Departure Program agreed to by the United States and Vietnam in 1980. If relations with Vietnam and Kampuchea (Cambodia) are regularized, this could lead to increased rates of emigration from both countries. Finally, because of the dismal employment situation in India, the emigration of highly educated Asian Indians is expected to continue for many more years.

The various effects of these forces for change make any attempt to project Asian immigration a rather risky proposition. While projections up to the year 2000 may be reasonably reliable, those that go much beyond this time are probably no better than sheer guesses.

Prospects and Implications for Higher Education

The prospects and implications of Asian demographics for higher education must be discussed in the context of the demographic and other changes that have been described in the previous sections.

Educational Equity and Affirmative Action. The changing demographics of the college-age population will necessitate much greater efforts by institutions of higher education to promote educational equity. From the experience gained in the past twenty years with educational equity programs in higher education, it has become clear that underprepared minority students can succeed academically if they are provided with additional assistance to overcome their academic deficiencies. Most institutions have tried to meet the needs of these students by providing them with a variety of support services, such as diagnostic testing, counseling, tutoring, and social and cultural events.

While black and Hispanic students will be the primary focus of such educational equity efforts, Asian students also have special needs that should be recognized and addressed by institutions of higher education. Perhaps their greatest and most urgent need is to improve their reading, writing, and speaking skills in English. According to a study by Ramist and Arbeiter (1984), almost 30 percent of the Asian students who took the Scholastic Aptitude Test in 1982–83 indicated that English was not their best language. This result is hardly surprising in view of the large numbers of Asian students who are immigrants or the children of recent immigrants. Improving the English proficiency of these students will require special efforts by institutions of higher education.

Studies have also shown that a disproportionate number of Asian students pursue degrees in the technical/scientific disciplines. At the same time, there is an underrepresentation of Asian students in fields such as the humanities and education. This tendency of Asian students to pursue degrees in the technical and scientific disciplines has been attributed to cultural orientation, the influences of schooling, and racial discrimination

(Watanabe, 1973; Sue and Frank, 1973). Precollege and in-college counseling programs are needed to assist Asian students in exploring a wider range of career options.

A problem that Asian students appear to share with other minority students is the racial bias and discrimination they face on college campuses. Such incidents appear to be on the rise on campuses across the country (Greene, 1987). Asian students often suffer extreme psychological stress and alienation when they experience racial bias. As a consequence, their academic performance may be detrimentally affected — sometimes to such an extent that they are forced to drop out of school. Institutions of higher education must begin to address this serious problem by instituting programs in cross-cultural psychological counseling, hiring Asian counselors, and raising the racial awareness and sensitivity of the entire campus community through workshops and staff training programs (Loo and Rolison, 1986).

In addition to these educational equity issues, Asian Americans also face problems in affirmative action. As noted earlier, Asians appear to be well represented on the faculties of most institutions of higher education. However, American-born Asians are still underrepresented on these faculties and are outnumbered ten to one by foreign-born Asians (Maxfield, 1981; Vetter and Babco, 1987). Asian women, both American-born and foreign-born, also are still underrepresented. Furthermore, Asian faculty generally earn lower salaries than their white counterparts, and only a few Asians have been appointed to high-level administrative positions. Institutions of higher education must become more sensitive to these problems and pursue affirmative action more vigorously on behalf of Asian Americans.

Admissions Controversy. Over the past five years, a heated controversy has arisen over the issue of whether some of the most prestigious institutions of higher education have imposed unofficial "quotas" on the numbers of Asian American students they will admit. Athough the 1980 census found that Asian Americans constituted 6 percent of California's population and 2 percent of the total U.S. population, in the fall of 1986 Asian American students constituted 26.5 percent of the freshman class at the University of California, Berkeley, 33 percent of the freshman class at the University of California, Irvine, and 8 to 19 percent of the freshmen at UCLA, Stanford, Harvard, Yale, Brown, and MIT (Nakao, 1987). These high percentages have apparently created considerable concern in these institutions that Asian students may be "overrepresented" and may be upsetting the "ethnic balance" of the student population (Salholz, 1987; Hassan, 1986–87). Many Asian Americans believe it was not coincidental that most of these institutions revised their admissions criteria in the past two to three years in ways that work to the disadvantage of Asian students.

Asian American individuals and community groups that have investigated the matter have found that though Asian applications to these institutions have increased substantially since 1983, the number of Asian students admitted by most of the institutions has remained about the same or has even decreased. Furthermore, they have found that a significantly larger proportion of white than Asian applicants are admitted. More specifically, the admissions rate for Asian students was found to be anywhere from 65 to 85 percent of the admissions rate for white students. Yet, the combined Scholastic Aptitude Test scores of the admitted Asian students were found to be as much as 112 points higher than those of the white student admittees (Bunzel and Au, 1987).

In regard to the issue of the "overrepresentation" of Asian students, institutional officials appear to be taking the position that since Asian Americans constitute only 2.1 percent of the total U.S. population, they should be considered overrepresented if their proportion of the student enrollment in an institution substantially exceeds this percentage. Such a position can be seriously questioned for at least two reasons. First, it presumes that affirmative action was instituted merely to maintain some sort of "ethnic balance" when, in fact, it was actually implemented to overcome the effects of past discrimination against certain groups in our society. These effects were most clearly manifested in patterns of segregation or exclusion, such as the underrepresentation of minorities in higher education. It was convenient and practical, therefore, to gauge the effectiveness of affirmative action efforts by determining the extent to which the proportion of minorities in institutions of higher education was increasing, that is, the extent to which ethnic balance was being achieved. However, when that proportion for a given minority group reaches or exceeds its proportion in the general population, it may be presumed in some, but not all, cases that parity has been reached and affirmative action efforts are no longer needed for that group. At this point, it would seem reasonable to adopt a "color-blind" admissions policy and admit both whites and members of that minority group on the same basis, that is, by using admissions criteria that do not discriminate against either group.

There is a second major flaw in the argument for maintaining ethnic balance. Even the so-called overrepresentation of a group does not necessarily imply that parity has been reached by that group. If that reasoning were accepted, institutions of higher education should also be concerned about the overrepresentation of blacks in athletic programs or the overrepresentation of women in certain degree programs, such as education, nursing, and home economics, and impose limits on their enrollments in these programs. In fact, however, it is well recognized that blacks and women are overrepresented in these fields precisely because of the patterns of discrimination they have faced historically. In the same way, as discussed in an earlier section, Asian Americans are overrepresented in higher education because they have tried to overcome the barriers of discrimination through education. Their overrepresentation does not mean they have yet overcome these barriers.

These admissions issues should be addressed objectively and fairly and with some urgency by institutions of higher education. As the projections presented earlier indicated, Asian student enrollments in higher education could double over the next ten to twelve years and come to constitute as much as 7 percent of the total college student population. Consequently, the controversy over Asian admissions could become even more heated and acrimonious in the absence of well-reasoned, equitable, and clearly articulated policies by institutions of higher education. As argued above, a policy based on maintaining ethnic balance does not seem reasonable once a minority group has reached parity. Moreover, in the case of Asian Americans, the differences in the socioeconomic status of the various Asian ethnic groups are so great that it may not make sense to apply the same policy to all these groups.

Summary

Asian Americans are now the fastest growing ethnic group in the nation. In 1985, the Asian American population was estimated to be over 5 million, or 2.1 percent of the total population. They appear to enjoy a relatively high socioeconomic status, but a detailed analysis of the data revealed that their success is problematic and that major differences exist between the various Asian groups. The educational achievements of Asian Americans have been just short of phenomenal, leading many to refer to them as the "model minority." However, the model minority image conceals the many problems that continue to face Asian Americans.

Demographic projections have indicated that Asian immigration will continue at a high rate, adding as many as four million more people to the Asian American population over the next ten to twelve years. The Asian American population is projected to grow to nearly ten million by 2000 and will make up almost 4 percent of the total population. Asian student enrollments in higher education are also expected to increase, possibly climbing to nearly 900,000 and coming to represent 7 percent of all students.

These demographic projections may be significantly affected by a number of societal forces. The growing international trade with Pacific Rim countries is already having a major societal impact and will have a profound effect on all sectors of our society, including institutions of higher education. A wide range of developing economic and political forces in Asia could also affect Asian immigration.

These demographic changes and societal forces have important implications for the future of higher education. The nature of higher education has already been changed in some profound ways, and even greater changes are on the horizon. Institutions of higher education will have to greatly increase their efforts to promote educational equity and affirmative action, and they must begin to address the controversy over the admission of Asian students in a forthright and equitable way.

References

Arnold, F., Minocha, U., and Fawcett, J. T. "The Changing Face of Asian Immigration to the United States." In J. T. Fawcett and B. V. Carino (eds.), *Pacific Bridges: The New Immigration from Asia and the Pacific Islands.* New York: Center for Migration Studies, 1987.

Boodman, S. G. "Korean Americans: Pursuing Economic Success." *Washington Post,* July 13, 1978, p. 1.

Bouvier, L. F, and Agresta, A. J. "The Fastest Growing Minority." *American Demographics,* 1985, *7,* 31–33, 46.

Bunzel, J. H., and Au, J.K.D. "Diversity or Discrimination? — Asian Americans in College." *Public Interest,* Spring 1987, pp. 49–62.

Cabezas, A. Y. *A View of Poor Linkages Between Education, Occupation, and Earnings for Asian Americans.* San Francisco: ASIAN Inc., 1977.

Chun, K.-T. "The Myth of Asian American Success and Its Educational Ramifications." *IRCD Bulletin,* 1980, *1* and *2,* 1–12.

Coleman, J. S., and others. *Equality of Educational Opportunity.* Washington, D.C.: U.S. Government Printing Office, 1966.

Evangelauf, J. "Minorities' Share of College Enrollments Edges Up, as Number of Asian and Hispanic Students Soars." *Chronicle of Higher Education,* Mar. 9, 1988, pp. A33–36.

Gardner, R. W., Robey, B., and Smith, P. C. "Asian Americans: Growth, Change, and Diversity." *Population Bulletin,* 1985, *40* (entire issue).

Greene, E. "Asian Americans Find U.S. Colleges Insensitive, Form Campus Organizations to Fight Bias." *Chronicle of Higher Education,* Nov. 18, 1987, pp. A1, A38–40.

Hassan, T. E. "Asian American Admissions: Debating Discrimination." *College Board Review,* 1986–87, *142,* 18–21, 42–46.

Immigration and Naturalization Service. *Statistical Yearbook of the Immigration and Naturalization Service, 1985*. Washington, D.C.: U.S. Department of Commerce, 1986.

"Japanese-U.S. Outdo Horatio Alger." *Los Angeles Times*, Oct. 17, 1977, p. I1.

Kaufman, P. "Trends in Elementary and Secondary Public School Enrollment." In J. D. Stern and M. F. Williams (eds.), *The Condition of Education*. Washington, D.C.: Center for Education Statistics, 1987.

Kraus, J. "Colleges Must Prepare Now for the Enrollment Crash of 1990." *Chronicle of Higher Education*. Jan. 6, 1988, p. B2.

Lockwood, C., and Leinberger, C. B. "Los Angeles Comes of Age." *Atlantic Monthly*, 1987, *261*, 31–56.

Loo, C., and Rolison, G. "Alienation of Ethnic Minority Students at a Predominantly White University." *Journal of Higher Education*, 1986, *57*, 58–77.

Maxfield, B. D. *Employment of Minority Ph.D.'s: Changes over Time*. Washington, D.C.: National Academy of Sciences, 1981.

Muscatine, C. "Dimensions/Challenges: Coherence in a New Context." In *Addresses and Proceedings of the 61st Annual Meeting of the Western College Association: Educational Coherence in a Multicultural Society*. Long Beach, Calif.: Western College Association, 1985.

Nakao, A. "Thorny Debate over UC: Too Many Asians?" *San Francisco Examiner*, May 3, 1987, pp. A1, A12.

"The New Whiz Kids." *Time*, Nov. 30, 1987, pp. 42–51.

Oxnam, R. B. "Why Asians Succeed Here." *New York Times Magazine*, Nov. 30, 1986, pp. 74–75, 88–89.

Pacific Rim Task Force. *California and the Pacific Rim: A Policy Agenda*. Sacramento: California Economic Development Corporation, 1986.

Peterson, W. "Success Story, Japanese American Style." *New York Times Magazine*, Jan. 9, 1966, pp. 20–21.

Peterson, W. "Chinese and Japanese Americans." In T. Sowell (ed.), *Essays and Data on American Ethnic Groups*. Washington, D.C.: Urban Institute, 1978.

Ramist, L., and Arbeiter, S. *Profiles, College-Bound Seniors, 1982*. New York: College Entrance Examination Board, 1984.

Salholz, E. "Do Colleges Set Asian Quotas?" *Newsweek,* Feb. 9, 1987, p. 60.

Snyder, T. D. *Digest of Education Statistics, 1987.* Washington, D.C.: Center for Education Statistics, 1987.

Stern, J. D., and Williams, M. F. (eds.), *The Condition of Education.* Washington, D.C.: Center for Education Statistics, 1987.

"Success Story of One Minority Group in U.S." *U.S. News & World Report,* Dec. 26, 1966, pp. 73–76.

"Success Story: Outwhiting the Whites." *Newsweek,* June 21, 1971, pp. 24–25.

Sue, D. W., and Frank, A. C. "A Typological Approach to the Psychological Study of Chinese and Japanese American College Males." *Journal of Social Issues,* 1973, *29,* 129–148.

Sung, B. L. *Chinese Manpower and Employment.* Washington, D.C.: U.S. Department of Labor Manpower Administration, 1975.

Suzuki, B. H. "Education and the Socialization of Asian Americans: A Revisionist Analysis of the 'Model Minority' Thesis." *Amerasia,* 1977, *4,* 21–51.

Tsang, S.-L., and Wing, L. C. *Beyond Angel Island: The Education of Asian Americans.* ERIC/CUE Urban Diversity Series, 1985, no. 90.

U.S. Bureau of the Census. *Race of the Population by States: 1980.* Supplementary Report, PC80-S1-3. Washington, D.C.: U.S. Department of Commerce, 1981.

U.S. Bureau of the Census. *Asian and Pacific Islander Population by State: 1980.* Supplementary Report, PC80-S1-12. Washington, D.C.: U.S. Department of Commerce, 1983a.

U.S. Bureau of the Census. *General Social and Economic Characteristics.* 1980 Census of the Population, PC80-1-C. Washington, D.C.: U.S. Department of Commerce, 1983b.

U.S. Bureau of the Census. *Detailed Population Characteristics.* 1980 Census of the Population, PC80-1-D1-A. Washington, D.C.: U.S. Department of Commerce, 1984.

U.S. Bureau of the Census. *Statistical Abstract of the United States, 1987.* Washington, D.C.: U.S. Department of Commerce, 1986.

U.S. Commission on Civil Rights. *Social Indicators of Equality for Minorities and Women.* Washington, D.C.: U.S. Commission on Civil Rights, 1978.

U.S. Commission on Civil Rights. *Recent Activities Against Citizens and Residents of Asian Descent.* Clearinghouse Publication, no. 88. Washington, D.C.: U.S. Government Printing Office, 1986.

Uyematsu, A. "The Emergence of Yellow Power in America." In A. Tachiki and others (eds.), *Roots: An Asian American Reader.* Los Angeles: Asian American Studies Center, University of California, Los Angeles, 1971.

Vetter, B. M., and Babco, E. L. *Professional Women and Minorities: A Manpower Data Resource Service.* (5th ed.) Washington, D.C.: Scientific Manpower Commission, 1984.

Vetter, B. M., and Babco, E. L. *Professional Women and Minorities: A Manpower Data Resource Service.* (7th ed.) Washington, D.C.: Scientific Manpower Commission, 1987.

Watanabe, C. "Self-Expression and the Asian American Experience." *Personnel and Guidance Journal,* 1973, *51,* 390–396.

Wilson, R., and Melendez, S. E. (eds.). *Fourth Annual Status Report on Minorities in Higher Education.* Washington, D.C.: Office of Minority Concerns, American Council on Education, 1985.

Yu, W. "Asian Americans Charge Prejudice Slows Climb to Management Ranks." *Wall Street Journal,* Sept. 11, 1985, p. 35.

E/o chap. 5

pp 116-118 (DIT)

Chap.

6

Older Students

by *William F. Brazziel* (sp)

Increases in older students on campuses must be regarded as one of the more remarkable developments in higher education in recent years. The average student on the campuses of the colonial colleges was about fifteen years old. On many of today's campuses the average age is nearly twice that. Some 40 percent (over five million) of all college students are now older students — twenty-five years of age and over. Last year these students walked away from commencement exercises with 37 percent of the bachelor's degrees (U.S. Department of Education, Center for Education Statistics, 1987), and this proportion can be expected to grow in the years ahead.

Adult Population

Put simply, adults are the fastest growing segment of all the population groups in higher education. Population growth for any group is a function of fertility, mortality, immigration, and emigration. Exogenous factors such as the economy and technological changes affect all these variables. They hasten or slow the building of population, encourage individuals to form families or compel them to forgo doing so for extended periods of time, and play a key role in fertility and mortality rates.

For example, if immigration establishes a population base and emigration is not severe, fertility becomes the key factor in population expansion. This has been the American experience (Brazziel, forthcoming). Figure 6.1 illustrates that the influenza epidemic of 1920, the stock market crash of 1929, the approval of the sale of oral contraceptives, and the legalization of abortions coincided with decreases in fertility, while the end of World War II in 1945 and the beginning of the echo boom (children of baby boomers) in 1976 coincided with sharp increases in fertility. *Fig 6.1*

In fact, much more than coincidence is involved here. The influenza epidemic took many lives and resulted in low birth cohorts. The stock market crash and the Great Depression discouraged family formation and depressed cohort sizes for over a decade. The seven years of unrivaled economic growth following World War II encouraged family formation, and large birth cohorts came to be the norm. In sum, prior exogenous factors determined the cohort sizes of today. For example, the small cohorts from 1932 to 1937 (during the Depression years) made for small fifty- to fifty-five-year-old cohorts in the late 1980s.

In *Birth and Fortune,* Easterlin (1980) has analyzed the ups and downs of fertility and cohort size that result from certain exogenous factors. According to Easterlin's Life Chance Theory, perceptions of chances for a happy prosperous life (a good life chance) lead to family formation, high fertility rates, and large birth cohorts. Perceptions of the opposite (a poor life chance) lead to limited family formation, low fertility rates, and low birth cohorts.

Perceptions of life chances as good or poor, according to Easterlin, are determined by the interaction of the cohort size with economic conditions. Perceptions of good life chances abound when small birth cohorts come of age. Because these cohorts are small, workers are scarce. Jobs are thus plentiful and wages are high because the law of supply and demand pushes them up. As a result, young people perceive their life chances as good. They form families, fertility rates rise, and large birth cohorts are the order of the day. The opposite occurs when these large cohorts come of age. This results in an oversupply of workers, and young people experience difficulty in getting ahead. Because perceptions of poor life chances abound, young people

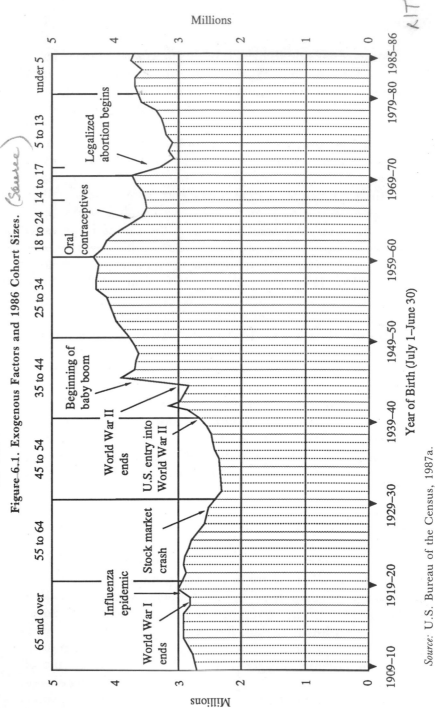

Figure 6.1. Exogenous Factors and 1986 Cohort Sizes.

Source: U.S. Bureau of the Census, 1987a.

delay family formation, fertility rates fall, and low birth cohorts are the result.

According to Easterlin, the cycle repeats itself from one generation to the next. The baby-boom and baby-bust generations are cases in point. The former were progeny of parents from small birth cohorts that benefited as no other generation has from economic growth and opportunity. The parents of the baby boomers were a small cohort, born during the Depression era, and they found themselves in great demand as adult workers in the boom years after World War II. They perceived their life chances as good and produced a dramatically larger generation of children. In contrast, their progeny — the baby boomers — had, and are still having, difficulty entering and moving ahead in the work force. Results: delayed family formation, low fertility, and small birth cohorts. This is especially true of individuals born during the last half of the baby boom. However, baby-bust youngsters now take their pick among the fast-food jobs and marvel at the horror stories their parents tell about the difficulties they had in getting into college. The mailboxes of these young people overflow with brochures from colleges inviting them to enroll.

The older population is increasing. Baby-boom children are now moving into their middle years, and the echo boom is just beginning. Figure 6.2 displays the progression of the former in graphic terms. Demographers use the concept of "a pig in a python" to describe the progression of this remarkably large cohort through life. The baby boom began in 1946 and ended in 1964. Nearly 80 million children were born during this period, over a third more than would normally be expected. The oldest baby boomer is now forty-three and the average boomer is thirty-three. At the height of the baby boom, 4.3 million children were born in one year (1957), nearly twice as many as were born in 1937, near the middle of the Depression. Figure 6.2 indicates that the cohorts between thirty-five and forty-four are now the fastest growing of all age groups and that they will make up the largest cohort for the next two decades. The pig, we might say, is simply moving farther along in the python.

Cohort size dropped to 3.1 million children at the lowest point of the baby-bust years (1973). Cohort size has since climbed to 3.8 million, but this is deceptive. The increase is almost entirely due to the reproduction rate among huge cohorts of the baby boom itself. In reality, a very large cohort—the baby boomers—is having fewer children and not even replicating its own numbers. In point of fact, overall fertility rates were at their lowest point (1.8 children per family) since the Depression.

Decennial census data indicate a total U.S. population of 241 million as of July 1, 1985, an increase of 6.4 percent from 1980. The median age of Americans—31.8—is up from 30 in 1980 and 27.9 in 1971 (U.S. Bureau of the Census, 1987a). This too reflects the aging of the baby-boom cohort.

The sixty-five-and-over population is growing rapidly because of advances in health care. As noted in figure 6.2, this group will grow enormously over the next twenty-five years when baby boomers reach this age. By 2030, more than 21 percent of all Americans will be sixty-five and over. Figure 6.2 also indicates the troughs ahead for the adult population years. The first includes the current fourteen-to-seventeen-year-old cohort that was born near the lows of the baby-bust years. The second consists of the under-five cohort, which has shown a small increase for each year since 1980. Finally, the five-to-thirteen-year-old cohort makes up a third trough. FIG. 6.2

What it all adds up to is this: There will be fewer young people and an abundance of older people in America in the years ahead. This bodes well for older student enrollment on campuses.

As can be seen from the data in Table 6.1, the fastest growing segment of the population in the last five years was the cohort between thirty-five and forty-four years of age. In contrast, the cohort under five years of age showed a 10.9 percent increase, an indication indeed that the baby boomers are starting to have children. The timing is a reflection of a generation of women who decided to delay childbearing owing to late marriages, careers, and, no doubt, perceptions of poor life chances. Hospitals have even set aside "Now or Never Wards" for these women, many of whom are thirty-five and older.

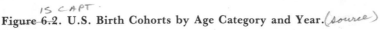

Figure 6.2. U.S. Birth Cohorts by Age Category and Year. (source)

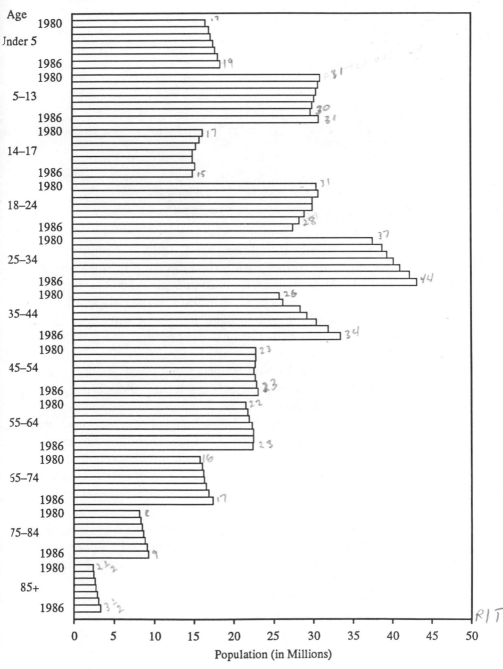

Source: U.S. Bureau of the Census, 1987a.

Table 6.1. U.S. Population by Selected Age Cohorts (in Thousands). *(source*

Age Cohorts	1986	1980	% Change
Cohorts Totals	241,596	227,061	6.4
Under 5 years	18,128	16,348	10.9
5 to 13 years	30,346	31,159	-2.8
14 to 17 years	14,797	16,249	-8.9
18 to 24 years	27,973	30,289	-7.6
25 to 34 years	42,984	37,259	15.4
35 to 44 years	33,143	25,698	29.0
45 to 54 years	22,822	22,806	0.1
55 to 64 years	22,230	21,703	2.4
65 to 74 years	17,325	15,581	11.2
75 to 84 years	9,051	7,729	17.1
85 years +	2,796	2,240	24.8

Source: U.S. Bureau of the Census, 1987a.

Between July 1, 1985, and July 1, 1986, 3.7 million children were born, net immigration (immigration minus emigration) was 613,000, and about 2 million people died. The population thus grew by 1 percent (2.3 million). Annual population growth of this magnitude has been the norm since 1980 and is expected to continue for the next decade or so (U.S. Bureau of the Census, 1987c).

As the large baby-boom cohorts reach the mortality years, however, and the baby-bust cohorts reach the childbearing years in greater number, there will be further population declines unless fertility rates among the baby-bust cohorts increase, immigration is moderate to heavy, or breakthroughs in science enable people to live longer. The population replacement rate for America is 2.1 children per family, which is 0.3 children above the current average (the extra 0.1 is required to compensate for mortality).

Data in Table 6.2 suggest that a population decline—or at least a population plateau—can be expected. These data forecast a cresting of birth cohort size in 1990, when 3.8 million children will be born. Cohort size will then fluctuate: There will be 3.4 million births in 2000, 3.6 million in 2010, and 3.5 million in 2030. Cohort size will decline to 3.4 million in 2080 and then level off. Deaths will begin to approximate births in 2030 and exceed births in 2050. As shown in Table 6.2, moderate immi-

IS CAPT.

Table 6.2. Population Projections, 1990–2080 (in Thousands). *(source)*

Year	Births	Deaths	Population[a]	Population[b]
1990	3,826	2,164	247,968	249,657
2000	3,494	2,363	263,896	283,238
2010	3,673	2,634	276,642	296,597
2030	3,546	3,434	292,780	304,807
2050	3,517	3,957	292,052	308,488
2080	3,434	3,878	285,692	310,762

NOTE [a]Estimates based on low net migration rates. *R/ Table*
NOTE [b]Estimates based on medium immigration rates. *R/ Table*
Source: U.S. Bureau of the Census, 1987a.

gration rates (net = 450,000) will result in gradual population increases through 2080, while low immigration rates (net = 250,000) will result in population decreases. Thus immigration will once more become a key factor in the population growth of the United States. Recent net immigration has been healthy (600,000 annually), and this may preclude an overall decline in the population. *Table 6.2*

Of course, many exogenous factors could intrude to cause forecasters to modify these projections. Fertility rates could increase and breakthroughs in medicine could increase longevity. Or both fertility and immigration could fall if serious economic dislocations result in low perceptions of life chances. People already living in the United States might hesitate to have children, and emigrants might hesitate to come here. Only time will tell.

But let us return to the population base in place. For those interested in the education of older students, the market for the next fifty years or so is already here. Attempts to understand and forecast older student enrollment have been futile until recently because no historical data on which to base these forecasts existed. The situation has changed, however, and models for such forecasting are beginning to appear.

Forecasting Older Student Enrollment

Older cohort participation matrixes (OCPM) represent one of the first models for forecasting older student enrollment and the very first model that enables state and local forecasters to estimate enrollment and institutional market share (Brazziel, 1987). OCPM utilizes the historical data on participation rates of older students in college as compiled by the U.S. Census Bureau in its Series P-20 population surveys. The bureau has collected these data for over a decade now, and participation rates have been sufficiently consistent to allow for forecasts.

The bureau collects these data annually by interviewing a stratified random sample of approximately 60,000 American families (U.S. Bureau of the Census, 1984b). The bureau also works closely with the Center for Education Statistics of the U.S. Department of Education. This unit collects data from colleges and universities directly through its Higher Education General Information Survey (HEGIS). HEGIS has recently been expanded to include both older students and students enrolled in vocational schools and will soon be renamed Integrated Postsecondary Education Data System (IPEDS) to reflect this change.

While both data collection systems are good, the effort to make final head counts jibe can be interesting. The standard error in random sampling, coupled with the human errors inevitably found in college and university reporting systems, preclude an exact match, of course. Series P-20 surveys also systematically exclude certain individuals. The surveys are limited to households, they do not count overseas military personnel taking courses, and they undercount military personnel stationed at U.S. bases who are taking courses. In contrast, HEGIS data account for all military personnel directly through reports made by institutions. Series P-20 surveys also exclude foreign students. Fortunately, these students are included in HEGIS data.

For OCPM and the other forecasting models that will surely follow, the P-20 data are essential. Participation rates are disaggregated according to age group, and stochastic forecasts are thus possible. HEGIS cannot provide such disaggregation, nor will the new IPEDS system. The aim for the researcher is to minimize the distance between totals.

OCPM begins with a population base that includes birth cohort data for all individuals likely to take a credit course at a college or university over a particular time frame. However, since older student participation in higher education drops sharply after age fifty-five, a population base consisting of sixty-six cohorts would encompass most of the individuals who would be interested in pursuing a college education. There are rare exceptions, of course. Two years ago, for example, a ninety-two-year-old Nebraska man earned a Ph.D. His dissertation had to do with the wagon train his grandfather joined to get to the state. Our data omit such people.

The sixty-six cohorts accounting for the population loss would include births from 1921 to 1986. Much of the earlier discussion of population variation due to exogenous factors is reflected in the birth numbers of these cohorts. A summary of these factors follows:

- Influenza epidemic, 1920: small birth cohorts
- Depression, 1930 to 1942: small birth cohorts
- Depth of Depression, 1937: smallest birth cohort
- End of World War II, 1945: large birth cohorts, baby boom
- Crest of baby boom, 1957: largest birth cohort
- Oral contraceptive approval, 1964: small birth cohort
- Legalization of abortion in several states, 1972: very small cohorts
- *Roe* v. *Wade,* 1973: nadir of baby bust, smallest birth cohort
- Echo boom begins, 1974: larger birth cohorts

A population base does not a forecast make, of course. The next step in modeling is to create a market base. This is done by aggregating cohorts by age to comprise a total of prospective adult students in higher education in any given year. Age twenty-five is used as a base year in this exercise. Table 6.3 presents a market base that includes sixty-five cohorts (1921 to 1985) aggregated by age groups by year. It can be seen that the market base for 1988 includes 155 million older people. This increases to 168 million for 1994 and 172 million for 1998. *P. 126 Table 6.3*

Unfortunately, a market base does not a forecast make either. Theoretically, all the individuals in the base could show up at the registrar's window. But of course only a small proportion will actually do so. This number is shown in Table 6.4. It

'S CAPT .

Table 6.3. Older Student Market Base:
Projected Older Population Cohorts Matrix, 1980–1998 (in Thousands) (NOTE)

Age	1980	1984	1988	1994	1998
25	4,104	4,298	4,098	3,571	3,136
26	4,078	4,250	4,167	3,502	3,256
27	3,965	4,370	4,268	3,521	3,559
28	3,847	4,218	4,258	3,606	3,718
29	3,751	4,104	4,298	3,760	3,571
30	3,554	4,078	4,250	4,027	3,502
31	3,560	3,965	4,370	4,098	3,521
32	3,535	3,848	4,218	4,167	3,606
33	3,700	3,751	4,104	4,266	3,760
34	3,289	3,554	4,076	4,256	4,027
ᵃ	97,290	105,070	113,470	127,080	137,120
Totals	134,673	145,506	155,577	168,850	172,776

— *Note:* Numbers are based on U.S. birth cohorts 25 . . . . ith years
earlier. They do not include students studying under temporary visas, and age
35 + cohorts are adjusted for mortality. R/T Table

NOTE ᵃData for 55 cohorts 35 years of age and over. R/T Table

was developed by multiplying the numbers in Table 6.3 by the
appropriate participation rates in higher education for the varying age groups.

For example, 10 percent of the market base of 4 million
twenty-five-year-olds in 1988 yields an estimated enrollment of
400,600 twenty-five-year-olds for 1988. Multiplying through for
the twenty-six-year-olds yields an estimated enrollment of 416,700
twenty-six-year-olds for 1988. After all years have been multi-
plied through, the totals for 1988 are aggregated for a total of
4.2 million as an estimated enrollment of older students for 1988.
The complete OCPM model (Brazziel, 1987) includes formulas
for forecasting state and service area enrollment. It also includes
a formula for forecasting institutional market share.

It should be noted that participation rates for the model
are based on 1984 Series P-20 population surveys. Thus, these
data represent a conservative estimate of older student enrollment in the years to come. Error is surely apt to be on the low
end, that is, underestimation is more likely than overestimation.

IS CAPT

Table 6.4. Older Student Enrollment Forecasts by Cohort, 1980–1998. *(sources - last entry)*

Participation Rates: 25–29 = 10%; 30–34 = 6%; 35+ = 82%	1980	1984	1988	1994	1998
25	410,400	429,800	409,800	357,100	313,600
26	407,800	425,000	416,700	350,200	325,600
27	396,500	430,700	426,800	352,100	355,900
28	384,500	421,800	425,800	360,600	371,800
29	375,100	410,400	429,800	376,000	357,100
30	213,240	244,680	255,000	241,620	210,120
31	213,600	237,900	258,420	245,880	211,260
32	212,100	230,820	253,080	250,020	216,360
33	222,000	225,060	246,240	256,480	225,800
34	197,340	212,240	244,630	255,480	241,620
a	797,780	861,574	930,454	1,042,056	1,125,368
Totals	3,830,560	4,129,974	4,296,724	4,087,536	3,954,328

R/T

Data source for participation rates: U.S. Census Bureau (1984b).

Data source for cohort size: National Center for Health Statistics, *Vital Statistics of the United States,* Annual Reports for 1921–86.

Note: Data are based on birth cohorts and older. Figures do not include students studying under temporary visas, students enrolled in noncredit courses, or overseas military personnel enrolled in courses. The data assume a constant participation rate for 1988–1998. *R/T Table*

NOTE ªData for 55 cohorts 35 years of age and older. *R/T Table*

Sources: U.S. Bureau of the Census, 1984b; National Center for Health Statistics, 1921–1986. *(DATA SOURCE)*

OCPM validation exercises utilizing older student enrollment data from Connecticut yielded a precision index of .95.

p. 127   It can also be noted from Table 6.4 that the forecasts exclude foreign students. Totals can be expanded by 400,000 or so to allow for these students, most of whom are older adults studying in American graduate schools. As noted earlier, military personnel enrolled in classes offered by American colleges and universities overseas are also excluded. Analysts at the Center for Education Statistics adjust total older student enrollment upward to account for both foreign students and overseas military students based on annual institutional reports (U.S. Department of Education, Center for Education Statistics, 1985). Finally, it can be noted from

Table 6.4 that a constant participation rate is assumed for the years 1988 to 1998. An increase in participation rates could result in enrollment rises, while a decrease would cause declines. Participation rates thus become central in forecasting older student enrollment in the years ahead. Table 6.4

p. 128   Nineteen eighty-eight was the peak year for older student enrollment according to these forecasts. Large numbers of baby boomers are now past the years of heavy participation in higher education, and children from the baby-bust years are beginning to take their place. It can be noted, for example, that the cohorts with four million births all appeared between 1954 and 1964. Thus, as seen in Table 6.3, ten of these cohorts will be between twenty-five and thirty-four years of age in 1988. These are the ages of heavy participation in college for older students. Table 6.3 also shows that only five cohorts of four million can be found in the listings for 1994 and that only one can be found in 1998. Further, the smallest cohort of the baby bust makes its appearance in the listings in 1998. This is the twenty-five-year-old cohort with 3.1 million people who were born in 1973. Thus, while Table 6.3 totals indicate an ever larger market base of older prospects for the next decade, Table 6.4 indicates an ever smaller enrollment forecast. The older prospects will be with us, but they will no longer be in the high participation years. An equation of sorts may help in explaining this dynamic:

- Many large cohorts in high participation years = Large enrollments
- Many small cohorts in high participation years = Small enrollments

Variations of this theme may be developed once the basics become familiar. For example, large cohorts in low participation years, small cohorts in high participation years.

Again, however, exogenous factors can intrude to alter these projections, as can endogenous factors such as alterations in institutional mission and student attitudes. A discussion of each follows.

Precluding Factors. It is well to begin with endogenous and exogenous factors that might reduce older student enrollment. One factor that is seldom discussed is a change in the prevailing ethos regarding lifelong learning. Said differently, college for older students might simply go out of style. Things like this happen. Other ways of learning might come onto the scene. The Learning Connection, a profit-making corporation operating classes in large cities, is an example of a competitor that might reduce the participation of older students in higher education. Or people might simply lose interest. If this happens, the proportion of older students attending classes for the sheer joy of learning would be the first to go.

Women account for over two-thirds of all undergraduate enrollment among older students. Undergraduates, in turn, account for over 70 percent of older student enrollment. Many of these women are "returners," that is, students who left college early to raise a family and who are now returning for a degree. But women are no longer leaving college in large numbers for these reasons — or for any other reasons. Baccalaureate completion for women is now comparable to baccalaureate completion for men (U.S. Bureau of the Census, 1987a). The "returner" segment of the older student market base will certainly be affected in the years to come by this development.

Life chances for the baby-bust workers may become so attractive that striving for an edge through further study and more degrees and certifications may no longer be necessary. Some members of the older student population could indeed be labeled "strivers."

Enabling Factors. The ever upward progression of an educated adult population and work force and the reduction in high-paying jobs that require little advanced education might be the single most powerful factor in the maintenance of and even increases in older student enrollment. American education has been a huge success story. Over 80 percent of the individuals in the older student market base (individuals twenty-five years of age and over) have a high school diploma. Over

40 percent have been to college and over 20 percent hold a college degree (U.S. Bureau of the Census, 1987a). Something of a "tipping point" can occur in situations like this. Ten years ago, for example, the number of working wives began an upward progression. So did family income. Today an ever increasing number of wives work — many out of necessity, to keep pace with rises in family expenses. The median family income in 1986 was over $26,000 and 57 percent of the wives worked. Median income for families with working wives was over $34,000 (U.S. Bureau of the Census, 1987a). As more older people go to college, more older people may *have* to go to college. Like the situation for many working wives, a choice in the matter may simply disappear.

Colleges and universities themselves will be important forces for maintaining older student enrollments as they increasingly reach out to these individuals to compensate for baby-bust enrollment deficits. Schools that were heretofore completely uninterested in recruiting older students have developed thriving operations for them. They have also discovered marketing and dropped their inhibitions about using it. Of course, some of these programs for older students may be dropped when the echo-boom cohorts come on line in 1996 and younger students become more plentiful. In the meantime, however, many of these programs will be expanded. While older students have kept headcounts stable on campuses, many of these students only enroll for a course or two a year, and the number of full-time equivalent students continues to slide. More older students, taking more courses, will become the norm on many campuses.

Both corporate and military educational operations will expand the market base for older students by offering more courses and programs for them. The old adage that "the more education people get, the more education people want" will play a role here. In other words, many of these students will eventually enroll in baccalaureate programs on college campuses.

A million new teachers will be needed in the years to come to serve echo-boom children and to replace the large number of teachers who will be retiring. Recertified teachers who left the field — or who never taught — will fill many of these jobs. Most of these individuals will enroll in certificate renewal classes, and the ranks of the older students will swell as a result. Nursing presents a similar case. Severe shortages are already occurring in this field, and aging baby boomers will produce an even greater demand for health care and thus cause an ever greater shortage of nurses. There may be an influx of adults who want to upgrade their nursing credentials or acquire such credentials for the first time.

Implications for Colleges and Universities

Anything could happen. However, without changes in enabling or precluding factors, the following can be expected to occur:

1. The number of adults aged twenty-five to fifty-five in the United States eligible to attend college will increase throughout this century.
2. The number of adults in this age group who actually attend college peaked in 1988. It will continue to decline throughout the rest of the century because the baby boomers who dominate the nation's population are zooming past the peak adult enrollment ages.
3. This loss in adult students will produce its most serious consequences for higher education in the next five years, when the number of eighteen-year-olds will hit its lowest trough.
4. The regions of the country where the eighteen-year-old population will decline significantly will feel the loss of adult students most seriously. The Midwest and East will be hit the hardest (see Chapter Two).
5. Both the institutions most dependent on traditional-age students and those most dependent on adults will be affected by the loss of adult students, the former because they have no replacement population to fall back on and the latter because their clientele is declining. Thus, liberal arts colleges, nonflagship state universities, and community coleges will be most deeply hurt by this loss.

References

Brazziel, W. F. "Planning for Demographic Shifts in Colleges and Universities." *Research in Higher Education,* Nov. 1978, pp. 1–13.

Brazziel, W. F. "Correlates of Enrollment Maintenance in Liberal Arts Colleges." *College and University,* 1985a, *61,* 151–154.

Brazziel, W. F. "Waiting for the Older Student." *Congressional Record,* 1985b, *131* (39), E1247–1248.

Brazziel, W. F. "Forecasting Older Student Enrollment." *Journal of Higher Education,* 1987, *58* (2), 223–231.

Brazziel, W. F. "Coming to America." *American Visions,* forthcoming.

Easterlin, R. *Birth and Fortune.* New York: Basic Books, 1980.

Jones, L. *Great Expectations: America and the Baby-Boom Generation.* New York: Coward, McCann, & Geoghegan, 1980.

National Center for Health Statistics. *Vital Statistics of the United States.* Annual Reports, 1921–1986.

U.S. Bureau of the Census. *Demographic and Socioeconomic Aspects of Aging in the United States.* Series P-23 Population Surveys. Washington, D.C.: U.S. Government Printing Office, 1984a.

U.S. Bureau of the Census. *School Enrollment: Social and Economic Characteristics of Students.* Series P-20 Population Surveys. Washington, D.C.: U.S. Government Printing Office, 1984b.

U.S. Bureau of the Census. *Estimates of the Population of the United States, by Age, Sex, and Race.* Series P-25 Population Surveys. Washington, D.C.: U.S. Government Printing Office, 1987a.

U.S. Bureau of the Census. *Population Profile of the United States.* Series P-23 Population Surveys. Washington, D.C.: U.S. Government Printing Office, 1987b.

U.S. Bureau of the Census. *Projections of the Population of the United States, by Age, Sex, and Race.* Series P-23 Population Surveys. Washington, D.C.: U.S. Government Printing Office, 1987c.

U.S. Department of Education, Center for Education Statistics. *Projections of Education Statistics, 1992–93.* Washington, D.C.: U.S. Government Printing Office, 1985.

U.S. Department of Education, Center for Education Statistics. "Baccalaureate Recipients by Age: 1984–85." Unpublished data, 1987.

E10 Chap. 6
E10 Part 1

TART
p. 133 (no beep)

PART TWO

Thinking Realistically About Demographic Projections and Planning

p. 134 is blank

7

Demography
Is Not Destiny
in Higher Education

(sp)

Richard A. Easterlin

There is an old saying that if we can see further than our forebears it is because we stand on their shoulders. Sometimes, however, we fail to take advantage of historical experience, and our vision is correspondingly impaired. The word that went forth to colleges in the mid 1970s—prepare for retrenchment—is being spread once again, without asking how well the last round of advice worked out. Now, as then, this prescription is based on simple projections of the size of the college-age population. As we shall see, however, even brief consideration of theory and evidence suggests that such blind faith in naive demographics is unwarranted. Indeed, there is reason to believe that projections based only on the college-age population may be systematically biased—that changes in the college-age populations, whether up or down, tend to exaggerate the prospective change in college enrollments, because of compensating movements in college enrollment rates. Meaningful projections of college enrollments—that is, those that will enable policymakers to arrive at reasonably informed and balanced judgments—require attention to the outlook for college enrollment rates equal to that now being given to projections of college-age population. To elaborate

135

these points, the following chapter takes up recent forecasts, why these forecasts went wrong, and what can be done to improve them.

Between 1975 and 1985 the population of eighteen- and nineteen-year-olds fell over 10 percent. In the mid 1970s this development could be foreseen with virtual certainty, because all those destined to reach college entrance age in 1985 were already born and most were resident in the United States. As a result, most analysts at that time confidently predicted a severe drop in college enrollments by the mid 1980s (Boulding, 1975; Cyert, 1978; Keyfitz, 1978; Trow, 1976). Relying again on simple demographics, forecasters predicted substantial shifts in the ethnic mix of college students in favor of Hispanics and blacks.

How well did actual experience conform to expectations? The answer is, quite poorly. In 1985, the total college enrollment of eighteen- and nineteen-year-olds was only 1 percent below that of 1975 and the distribution of enrollment by ethnicity was virtually unchanged (Tables 7.1 and 7.2). Put differently, the

IS CAPT.

Table 7.1. Percentage Change in Population Aged 18–19 and College Enrollment of 18- and 19-Year-Olds, by Ethnicity, 1975–1985.

	Population	College Enrollment
All races	– 10.3	– 1.3
White non-Hispanic	– 14.5	– 1.8
Spanish origin	16.6	7.6
Black	4.1	– 0.4

R/T
P. 137 – Table 7.2

actual *1975* figures for college enrollments would have been a better predictor of 1985 enrollments, total and by ethnicity, than the projected college-age population of 1985. Table 7.1

Why were the forecasts so far off? The technical answer is that college enrollment *rates* of eighteen- and nineteen-year-olds, which the forecasts assumed would remain constant at 1975 levels, in fact changed markedly in a direction compensating for the population changes. The enrollment rate for the white non-Hispanic population rose by 15 percent, while the rates for

IS CAPT

Table 7.2. Percentage Distribution by Ethnicity
of College Enrollment of 18- and 19-Year-Olds, 1975 and 1985.

	1975	1985	% Change
All races	100.0	100.0	0
White non-Hispanic	87.2	86.7	-0.5
Spanish Origin	4.0	4.4	0.4
Black	8.8	8.9	0.1

R/T

blacks and Hispanics fell by 5 and 8 percent, respectively (Table 7.3). These movements in college enrollment rates virtually negated the projected effects on enrollments of movements in the college-age population. This observation, in itself, should make the case that the outlook for enrollment rates deserves attention equal to that given to the college-age population.

IS CAPT

Table 7.3. Percentage of Population Aged 18 and 19 Years
Enrolled in College, by Ethnicity, 1975 and 1985.

	1975	1985	% Change
All races	36.7	40.4	10.1
White non-Hispanic	39.4	45.3	15.0
Spanish Origin	24.1	22.2	-7.9
Black	25.3	24.1	-4.7

R/T

Of course, there may be some who feel that recent experience was idiosyncratic. Both theoretical reasoning and empirical analysis, however, suggest that this is not so. A critical assumption of enrollment forecasts that are based simply on the change in college-age population is that college enrollment rates are not themselves affected by the size of the college-age population. But enrollment rates, in fact, partly depend on the size of the college-age population—other things remaining constant, at the aggregate level a larger college-age population makes for lower enrollment rates, while a smaller college-age population makes for higher rates.

Several reasons for this relationship can be suggested. Recent work by a number of economists suggests that a surge in the young adult population depresses the returns from college education and vice versa (Freeman, 1979; Welch, 1979; Berger, 1984; Stapleton and Young, 1984). This implies that a decline in the young adult population would enhance the returns from a college education and stimulate increased enrollment rates. A second argument centers on the financial strains experienced by families who send children to college. If parents have two or more children in the college-age bracket at the same time, then the difficulties of financing college education are greater than when they have only one (Goldberg and Anderson, 1974). Thus, a decline in the college-age population such as that of the last decade would mean, other things remaining constant, that parents could more easily finance college educations for their children, because fewer of their children would be reaching college age at the same time. Third, there may be institutional responses to the expectation that applications will fall when the size of the college-age population is projected to decline. For example, admission standards may be lowered or the recruiting efforts of college admissions offices may be increased. The fact that Scholastic Aptitude Test scores have recently edged upward may raise doubts about any recent relaxation of admission standards. These scores, however, may also be inversely affected by the size of the youth population (Easterlin, 1978).

Empirical support for an inverse association between college enrollment rates and the size of the college-age population is provided by studies of the longer-term experience of both the United States and Japan. A multivariate analysis of American college enrollment rates in the period 1948 to 1976, done by the present writer and two colleagues, found a statistically significant inverse association between the size of the college-age population and college enrollment rates (Ahlburg, Crimmins, and Easterlin, 1981). A rapid rise in college enrollment rates in the 1950s was found to be due partly to the scarcity of college-age persons; the leveling off in the 1970s, partly to an upsurge in the college-age population. A similar inverse relationship has been reported for Japan during the period 1955 to 1984 (Atoh and Otani, 1988). Thus, over the long term, college enrollment rates have moved inversely with college-age population. In the past decade this inverse association has even characterized the *hold page)*

major ethnic groups. When these groups are ranked by size of change in the college-age population, the ordering, from low to high, is: white non-Hispanic, black, Hispanic. The rank ordering for the change in college enrollment rates is just the opposite (Table 7.4). *Table 7.4*

is capt.

Table 7.4. Percentage Change in Population and Enrollment Rate
of 18- and 19-Year Olds, 1975–1985, for Ethnic Groups
Ranked from Low to High by Population Change.

	(1) Population	(2) College Enrollment Rate
White non-Hispanic	– 14.5	15.0
Black	4.1	– 4.7
Spanish origin	16.6	– 7.9

College enrollment rates do not, of course, depend solely on the size of the college-age population. The multivariate analysis cited above also included — as independent variables that determine college enrollment rates — real family income, the intensity of the military draft in the period 1960 to 1972, and a measure of opportunities in the labor and marriage markets. The changing availability of financial aid, as well as the admission and recruiting policies of colleges, though not included in the study, also deserve attention. One would suppose that these circumstances would be especially relevant to explaining the previously noted differences in enrollment rate trends among blacks, Hispanics, and non-Hispanic whites. As another example, among females over age thirty-five, there is evidence suggesting that college enrollment rates have been significantly affected by divorce rates (Crimmins and Riddler, 1985). These and other determinants of college enrollment rates deserve careful study. This chapter emphasizes the size of the college-age population as a determinant of enrollment rates because once one recognizes this relationship, projections ignoring it are immediately called into question.

The lesson of the present discussion for college enrollment projections is a simple one: Projections cannot be based simply on the assumption that the enrollment rates of the college-age population will remain unchanged. Instead, meaningful projections must incorporate plausible assumptions about the outlook for enrollment rates together with that for the college-age population. At a minimum, a set of alternative projections, each based on different enrollment rate assumptions, might be developed, as is currently done for the government's population projections. For example, if the total college-age population were projected to decline, then a "low variant" projection of college enrollments might assume no change in enrollment rates, while medium and high variant projections would assume rate increases of progressively higher magnitude. (Because users gravitate toward medium variant projections, it should be clear from the foregoing discussion why that projection should *not* be one that assumes no change in enrollment rates.) Such projections would, at least, serve to warn educational policymakers against undue reliance on any single set of figures and promote more judicious consideration of alternative prospects.

But this is a minimum proposal. It would obviously be preferable to develop rate projections (again, in several variants) based on relevant empirical evidence. Such evidence might be provided by multivariate analyses of time-series or cross-sectional data that identify determinants of enrollment rates. Another (not mutually exclusive) approach would be to draw on surveys that measure the college aspirations of high school students (Johnston, Bachman, and O'Malley, 1988). Obviously, college educators and admissions personnel have knowledge and data that could inform such research.

None of this will be easy. But if the effort is not made, college administrators will continue to be led down the wrong path, assuming demographics is destiny.

References

Ahlburg, D., Crimmins, E., M. and Easterlin, R. A. "The Outlook for Higher Education: A Cohort Size Model of Enrollment of the College Age Population, 1948–2000." *Review of Public Data Use*, 1981, *9,* 211–227.

Atoh, M., and Otani, K. "Change in Age Composition and Its

Effects on the Youth Population." In United Nations Department of International Economic and Social Affairs, *Economic and Social Implications of Population Aging*. New York: United Nations, 1988.

Berger, M. C. "Cohort Size and the Earnings Growth of Young Workers." *Industrial and Labor Relations Review*, 1984, *37*, 582–591.

Boulding, K. "The Management of Decline." *Change*, 1975, *7*, 64.

Crimmins, E. M., and Riddler, E. W. "College Enrollment Trends Among the Population Thirty-Five and Older: 1972–1982 and Projections to 2000." *Educational Gerontology*, 1985, *11*, 363–385.

Cyert, R. M. "The Management of Universities of Constant or Decreasing Size." *Public Administration Review*, 1978, *38*, 344–349.

Easterlin, R. A. "What Will 1984 Be Like? Socioeconomic Implications of Recent Twists in Age Structure." *Demography*, 1978, *15*, 397–432.

Freeman, R. "The Effect of Demographic Factors on Age-Earnings Profiles." *Journal of Human Resources*, 1979, *14*, 289–318.

Goldberg, D., and Anderson, A. *Projections of Population and College Enrollments in Michigan, 1970–2000*. Lansing, Mich.: Governor's Commission on Higher Education, 1974.

Johnston, L. D., Bachman, J. G., and O'Malley, P. M. *Monitoring the Future: Questionnaire Responses from the Nation's High School Seniors, 1987*. Ann Arbor, Mich.: Survey Research Center, Institute for Social Research, 1988.

Keyfitz, N. "The Impending Crisis in American Graduate Schools." *The Public Interest*, 1978, *52*, 85–97.

Stapleton, D., and Young, D. "The Effect of Demographic Change on the Distribution of Wages, 1967–1990." *Journal of Human Resources*, 1984, *19*, 175–201.

Trow, M. "The Implications of Low Growth Rates for Higher Education." *Higher Education*, 1976, *5*, 377–396.

Welch, F. "Effects of Cohort Size on Earnings: The Baby-Boom Babies Financial Bust." *Journal of Political Economy*, 1979, *87*, S65–S97.

E/o Chap. 7

Pp 142-145 (DIT)

Chap. 8

Uses and Misuses of Demographic Projections: Lessons for the 1990s

by *Carol Frances* (SP)

Preparing for the future is the most important task that higher education has. People on college campuses all across the country are beginning to focus on the 1990s. But let us begin our inquiry by examining how well we did getting ready for the 1980s and by seeing what we can learn from that experience.

The major problem with planning for the 1980s was the use — and misuse — of demographic projections. Much of the planning for the 1980s was based on wrong assumptions and, as a result, much of that planning did more harm than good.

The purpose of this chapter is, first, to take another look at the projections of college enrollments made for the 1980s on the basis of demographic trends; second, to show what has actually happened to college enrollments since 1980; and third, to draw lessons from this experience to improve planning in higher education for the next decade.

Demographic Projections for the 1990s

Demographers claim that their projections of eighteen-year-olds, or eighteen- to twenty-four-year-olds, are likely to be correct ten to fifteen years out because, after all, the people have already been born and almost all of them will survive. For example, the people who will be eighteen to twenty-four in the year 2000 were born in the years from 1976 to 1982 and are already in the population. Many education planners then use these college-age population data with more confidence than they should to project college enrollments.

In the late 1970s and early 1980s the planners saw projected declines in the 1990s of over 20 percent in the eighteen-to-twenty-four-year-old age group, and on the basis of these demographic trends they projected significant college enrollment declines of up to 15 percent or more.

So far, however, total college enrollment has held steady or even increased in spite of declines in the college-age population. From 1980 to 1987, total college enrollment increased by 3.7 percent, while the eighteen-to-twenty-four-year-old population declined by 9.7 percent (Figure 8.1). *Fig 8.1*

One important part of the explanation is that the college-going rate of the eighteen-to-twenty-four-year-old group increased in the 1980s. Thus, although the college-age group got smaller, a larger percentage of that group enrolled in college — a phenomenon that is coming to be known as the cohort effect. Second, the decline in the enrollment of the traditional college-age population was much more than offset by the increase in enrollment of people twenty-five and over (Figure 8.2). *Fig 8.2*

There is a close connection between trends in the number of eighteen-year-olds and the number of first-time freshmen, but there is very little connection between total enrollment and the number of traditional college-age students.

Recent overall trends in college enrollment are already well known. But there are, in addition, some very interesting crosscurrents that may have significant implications for the 1990s. The next section analyzes the composition of enrollment change in the 1980s.

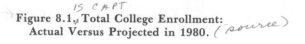

Figure 8.1. Total College Enrollment: Actual Versus Projected in 1980. (*source*)

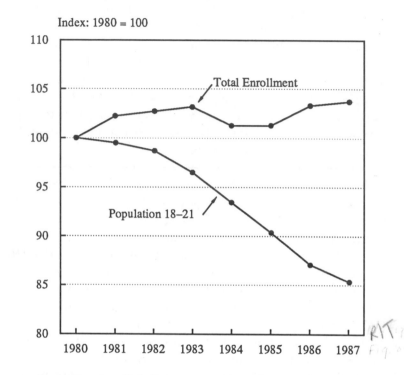

Source: Based on U.S. Department of Education and U.S. Department of Commerce data.

Why Have College Enrollments Gone Up in the 1980s?

Enrollment went up, not down, between 1980 and 1987. The increase in enrollment was 3.7 percent on the basis of total head counts and 2.7 percent in terms of full-time equivalent students.

The composition of the enrollment change is dramatically different, however, depending on how we view it. (The data on which the following summary is based are included in Tables 8.1 to 8.8 at the end of the chapter.) Here, we will look at the enrollment change from seven different viewpoints:

IS CAPT

Figure 8.2. Enrollment Change by Age, 1980–1986. (source)

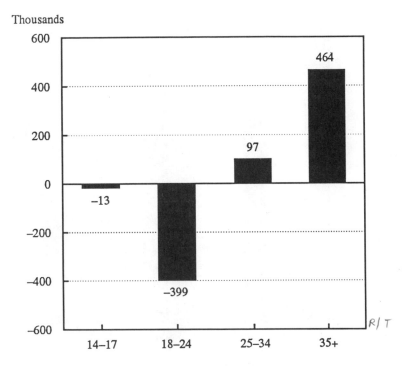

Thousands

464

97

−13

−200

−400

−399

−600

14–17   18–24   25–34   35+

R/T

Source: Based on U.S. Department of Education data.

By Full-Time/Part-Time Enrollment Status. Total enrollment increased not only on the basis of head counts but also
in terms of full-time equivalent students, because both full-time
and part-time enrollment increased. Part-time enrollment, however, accounted for almost three-fourths of the increase in total
enrollment from 1980 to 1987, because it grew almost four times
as fast as full-time enrollment since 1980 (Figure 8.3). Part-time
enrollment increased 6.5 percent while full-time enrollment increased 1.7 percent. P. 146 - Fig 8.3

By Gender. Women accounted for virtually all—98.4
percent—of the increase in college enrollment from 1980 to 1987.
As recently as 1970 there were 1.5 million, or one and a half

Figure 8.3. Enrollment Increase, 1980–1987. *(source)*

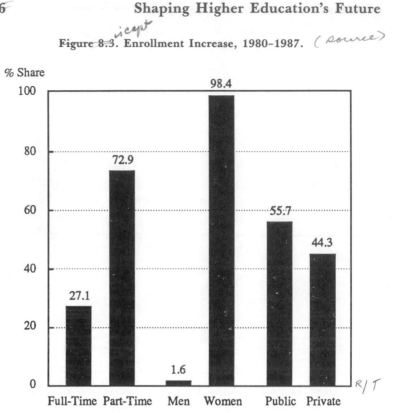

% Share

Source: Based on U.S. Department of Education data.

times, more men than women in college. Women started closing the gap at a rapid pace in the mid 1970s, and by 1979 they accounted for more than half of college enrollment. Then in the 1980s, while the enrollment of men jogged sideways, the enrollment of women continued to move upward. By 1987 there were almost 800,000 more women in college than men.

There are a larger number and percentage of women than men enrolled in college part-time; but even counting full-time equivalent students, more than half are women.

By Sector. The private colleges and universities gained a very significant share of the increase in enrollment between 1980 and 1987. While private institutions accounted for only about 22 percent of total enrollment in 1980, they accounted for 44 percent of the enrollment increase from 1980 to 1987. This is particularly noteworthy because when enrollment declines were projected for the 1980s, a corollary projection was frequently made that private institutions would be hit harder than public ones. In actuality, the opposite happened.

By Type of Institution. Colleges are often grouped by sector — public and private — and by type — university, other four-year, and two-year. In overall enrollment trends, universities fared less well than other four-year institutions. Private universities did less well overall than their public counterparts, while the other private four-year institutions had larger enrollment increases than their public counterparts.

Public institutions account for 97.8 percent of the two-year college enrollment, but they experienced slight declines of 1.4 percent over this period, while the private two-year colleges experienced small gains in the number of students but large gains in terms of percentage increases.

In analyzing trends in enrollment by sector, it is essential to differentiate not only between the public sector and the private sector but also between nonprofit private institutions and for-profit private institutions.

By far the fastest growing sector of higher education in the first half of the 1980s was the for-profit component of the private sector. The proprietary institutions accounted not only for more than two-thirds of the increase in enrollment in the private sector but also for more than one-half of the increase in total enrollment in all institutions of higher education over this period. The private religiously affiliated institutions accounted for about 40 percent of the private sector enrollment, and they also experienced a resurgence of enrollment over this period.

Those private institutions organized as independent non-profit colleges and universities maintained their enrollments, while in the public sector locally based institutions lost enrollment and the federal institutions, primarily the military academies, increased their enrollments between 1980 and 1987.

START NEW TRACK

By Undergraduate/Graduate Level. Contrary to projections for the 1980s, graduate enrollment grew faster than undergraduate enrollment, while first professional enrollment — primarily in law, medical, and dental schools — declined slightly.

Significantly, all the net growth in graduate enrollment from 1980 to 1987 was in the private sector. There was a gain of about 44,000 students in the private sector and a loss of close to 9,000 in the public sector, resulting in a shift of over 50,000 graduate students from the public to the private sector in the short space of seven years. The private colleges and universities accounted for more than 60 percent of the first professional enrollment in the 1980s, and they experienced even more modest declines in enrollment in this field than did the public colleges.

Something very interesting is going on at the undergraduate level. A lot of attention is focused on trends in first-time freshman enrollment, which decreased by 14.5 percent from 1980 to 1986. This is generally seen as a serious cause for alarm when the effects on future enrollment of the dent in the pipeline are taken into account.

But a different picture emerges when the rest of the facts are presented. While many people look at trends in first-time freshmen, hardly anybody looks at trends in the rest of undergraduate enrollment. Thus, while first-time freshman enrollment decreased by 374,000 from 1980 to 1986, other undergraduate enrollment increased by 696,000, for a net increase in total undergraduate enrollment of 322,000.

Something appears to be happening in the second, third, and fourth years of college, but we do not know yet whether it is positive or negative from the perspective of either the student or the institution. This increase after the freshman year could mean that there is an increase in retention, which would be a favorable trend, or it could mean students have to take a longer time to reach their educational objectives, going to college part-time because they can no longer afford to attend full-time, which would be an unfavorable trend.

By Age. Looking at enrollment trends for students grouped by age and gender, we find that the increase in full-time enrollment of women age thirty-five and over represents the most dramatic increase in enrollment. In 1980 about one of every eight women thirty-five and over was enrolled full time, but by the middle of the decade, close to one in four was enrolled full time.

By Race and Ethnicity. Some of the biggest news about recent enrollment trends is that 80 percent of the increase from 1980 to 1986 was accounted for by minority students and foreign students, while only 20 percent was accounted for by white non-Hispanic students.

At the same time, it has to be recognized that the term *minority students* was redefined for statistical purposes to include Asian students, who were not until recently identified separately. In fact, according to Department of Education data, the Asian enrollment in college more than doubled in the six years from 1980 to 1986 as a result of increase in enrollment both of Asians born here and of Asians who had immigrated to this country. In numbers and percentages, Asian enrollment increased more than that of any other major race or ethnic group (Figure 8.4). *Fig. 8.4 on p. 151*

College enrollment of Hispanics increased by about one-third over this period, while the enrollment of blacks decreased.

Lessons for the 1990s

The first lesson is, Don't trust demographers. Don't trust planners in demographer's clothing, either. One problem with allowing demographers to guide planning for higher education is that the models they use to project college enrollments are far too simple or too single-minded. Their enrollment projection models look like this: *a diagram*

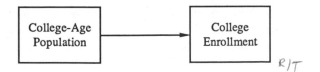

```
┌─────────────────┐        ┌─────────────────┐
│  College-Age    │───────▶│    College      │
│  Population     │        │   Enrollment    │
└─────────────────┘        └─────────────────┘
```
R/T

In fact, enrollment projection models should look more like this:

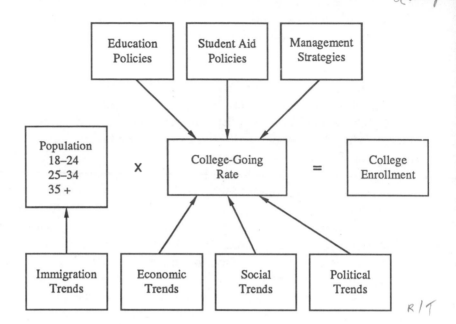

The second lesson is, Don't place too much trust in economists — especially ones who tell you that "the most basic statistic for understanding the future of American higher education is the number of births in the United States." This assertion is certainly no better than the premise that "the most basic statistic for understanding the future of American higher education is the fact that the more education people have, the more they want." Or, "the more education some people have, the more others need."

Actually, one of the most important factors in projecting college enrollment in the 1990s will be projection of college-going rates — specifically, projection of the speed at which the gap is closed between the college-going rates of whites and those of disadvantaged minorities. My work with enrollment projection models to the year 2015 leads me to the firm conclusion that whether college enrollments increase, hold steady, or decline in the 1990s will depend very heavily on whether the gap in

IS CAPT .

Figure 8.4. Enrollment Change, by Race, 1980–1986. *(source)*

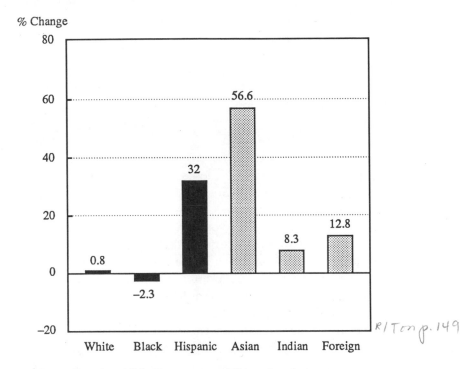

% Change

R/Tmp p. 149

White   Black   Hispanic   Asian   Indian   Foreign

Source: Based on U.S. Department of Education data.

college-going rates between white and disadvantaged minorities is closed 0, 20, 50, or 100 percent in five, ten, or fifty years.

A third lesson: When you do demographic trend analysis, look at all the relevant population trends. A serious problem with demographic planning in higher education is that demographers usually bring only some of their numbers to the table. Demographers who make enrollment projections usually talk about trends in the number of eighteen-year-olds or eighteen- to twenty-four-year-olds.

Instead, demographic analysis should include information about the trends for all the relevant population groups. For the purposes of making college enrollment projections, that means virtually all population groups. I was going to say except for the elderly, but the elimination of mandatory retirement in the next few years could make even that exception obsolete. For some colleges, then, it would be shortsighted to ignore the older age groups.

Considerable care must be taken in designating the population groups to use in demographic analysis to ensure that the ages included correspond as closely as possible to the educationally relevant categories for which college-going rates can be computed. This means that a census category of fifteen to twenty-four years of age, for instance, is too broad. It also means that a grouping of eighteen to twenty-four may be too broad if it is important to understand the considerable differences in the college-going behavior of those eighteen to nineteen, twenty to twenty-one, and twenty-two to twenty-four. Along with age groups, race and gender groups are also very important.

In the 1980s the decline in the eighteen-to-twenty-four-year-old population was offset in part by increases in the twenty-five-to-twenty-nine-year-old population. In the 1990s, both these age groups will turn down. Even the number of thirty- to thirty-four-year-olds will decline. Ah, the doom and gloomers gloat, we may have been wrong in the 1980s, but surely we will be vindicated in our projections of enrollment decline in the 1990s. Well, maybe so.

There may, indeed, be an enrollment decline driven by demographics in the mid 1990s. Yet the decline in the eighteen-to-twenty-four-year-old group will slow dramatically in the 1990s. There appears to have been a decrease of 15 percent in the traditional college-age group from 1980 to 1990. This compares with a decrease of only about 5 percent from 1990 to 2000. After a trough is reached in the middle of the decade, the trend will turn up again through the next several years.

The big demographic swing will be in the twenty-five-to-thirty-four-year-old group, which will go from a 16 percent increase in the 1980s to a 16 percent decrease in the 1990s. But the very large population group between thirty-five and sixty-four has experienced, and will continue to experience, huge increases: almost 20 percent in the 1980s and 24 percent in the 1990s.

There are more students in college aged thirty-five and over than there are students aged eighteen. The older age group will increase by roughly 20 million people in the 1990s — from about 85 million to about 104 million. College enrollments may well go down, but consider that a 0.5 percent increase in the college-going rate of this group could mean a 500,000 increase in college enrollments. To put these numbers into a historical context, from 1970 to 1985 the college-going rates of the population between thirty-five and sixty-four increased by 0.8 percent, which together with the increase in the numbers of people in this age group led to a growth in their college enrollment of close to one million.

I am neither a Pollyanna nor a riverboat gambler, but if I were going to put my money down, I would not bet on a significant enrollment decline in the 1990s even on the basis of demographic trends, let alone taking into consideration the expanding role of higher education as America's new basic industry.

A fourth piece of advice is to look at trends both in population and in college-going rates when making enrollment projections. The college-going rates incorporate the effects of trends in the larger educational, economic, social, and political environment. Demographic analysis is the place to start enrollment planning for the 1990s. It should not end there, however, because educational aspirations, social attitudes, economic trends, and public policies usually have as much effect on college enrollments as do demographic trends, and these other factors should be included prominently in analysis and planning.

Overemphasis on demographics and sometimes on just one slice of the demographics in higher education planning in the 1980s diverted attention from other serious problems, including the problem of inflation. Certain misguided planners, who looked at the demographics wearing blinders that narrowed their vision, intensified the fear of weakened demand for higher education and, consequently, of enrollment decline. This led colleges and universities to try to hold down tuition increases in the late 1970s while the costs that they could not control pushed upward. This contributed to delayed adjustments to inflation in the late 1970s and catch-up tuition increases in the 1980s.

Inflation eroded the resource base of higher education, extending across investments in human capital, physical capital, and financial capital, and this led colleges to depend more and more on borrowing. Paying back the loans will increase their fixed costs and increase their risks as they enter the 1990s.

Thus, the overemphasis on truncated demographics in the 1980s deflected attention from other pressing problems and postponed the search for solutions to them to the 1990s, when those problems may be even harder to deal with.

The final—and most important—lesson for enrollment planning is: Don't entrust planning for the 1990s to anyone who works primarily with numbers. The future will be shaped more by people who have ideas and values than by people who only know how to manipulate numbers.

My most fundamental concern about planning for the future based on demographics is that this kind of planning becomes passive. There is not much anybody can do about demographic trends but adapt to them. For higher education planners looking only at a decreasing number of eighteen- to twenty-four-year-olds, this has meant that the job to be done is the management of decline.

Alternatively, if the focus of planning efforts is on college-going rates and if attention is directed toward what can be done to increase the college-going rates of minorities, then there are action agendas—management strategies, social programs, and public policies that could make a difference.

is CAPT

Table 8.1 Composition of the Enrollment Change, 1980–1987 (in Thousands). (source)

	1980	1987	1980–1987	% Change	% Distribution of Increase
Total	12,097	12,544	447	3.7	100.0
Full-Time	7,098	7,219	121	1.7	27.1
Part-Time	4,999	5,325	326	6.5	72.9
Full-Time Equivalent	8,819	9,059	240	2.7	59.4

Uses and Misuses of Demographic Projections

Table 8.1. Composition of the Enrollment Change,
1980–1987 (in Thousands), Cont'd.

	1980	1987	1980–1987	% Change	% Distribution of Increase
Men	5,874	5,881	7	0.1	1.6
Women	6,223	6,663	440	7.1	98.4
Public	9,457	9,706	249	2.6	55.7
Private	2,640	2,838	198	7.5	44.3

E/o Table 8.1
Table 8.2

Source: U.S. Department of Education, Center for Education Statistics, 1988.

ii capt

Table 8.2. Composition of the Enrollment Change, by
Type of Institution, 1980–1985 (in Thousands).

	1980	1985	1980–1985	% Change	% Distribution of Increase
All Institutions	12,097	12,247	150	1.2	100.0
Universities	2,902	2,871	(31)	− 1.1	− 20.7
Other Four-Year	4,669	4,845	176	3.8	117.3
Two-Year	4,526	4,531	5	0.1	3.3
Public Institutions	9,457	9,479	22	0.2	14.7
Universities	2,154	2,141	(13)	− 0.6	− 8.7
Other Four-Year	2,974	3,068	94	3.2	62.7
Two-Year	4,329	4,270	(59)	− 1.4	− 39.3
Private Institutions	2,604	2,768	128	4.8	85.3
Universities	748	730	(18)	− 2.4	− 12.0
Other Four-Year	1,694	1,777	83	4.9	55.3
Two-Year	198	261	63	31.8	42.0

is capt

>Table 8.3. Composition of the Enrollment Change,
by Sector, 1980–1985 (in Thousands).

	1980	1985	1980–1985	% Change	% Distribution of Increase
All Institutions	12,097	12,247	150	1.2	100.0
Public	9,457	9,479	22	0.2	14.7
Federal	51	56	5	9.8	3.3
State	5,879	5,924	45	0.8	30.0
State and Local	2,361	2,439	78	3.3	52.0
State Related	155	148	(7)	– 4.5	– 4.7
Local	1,011	912	(99)	– 9.8	– 66.0
Private	2,640	2,768	128	4.8	85.3
Independent Nonprofit	1,522	1,530	8	0.5	5.3
Organized as Profit Making	112	196	84	75.0	56.0
Religiously Affiliated	1,006	1,042	36	3.6	24.0

E/o Table
Table 8.

> Table 8.4. *is capt* Composition of the Enrollment Change,
by Level, 1980–1985 (in Thousands).

	1980	1985	1980–1985	% Change	% Distribution of Increase
Total	12,097	12,247	150	1.2	100.0
Public	9,457	9,479	22	0.2	14.7
Private	2,640	2,768	128	4.8	85.3
Undergraduate	10,475	10,597	122	1.2	81.3
Public	8,441	8,478	37	0.4	24.7
Private	2,033	2,120	87	4.3	58.0
Graduate	1,343	1,376	33	2.5	22.0
Public	900	891	(9)	– 1.0	– 6.0
Private	442	486	44	10.0	29.3

Table 8.4. Composition of the Enrollment Change,
by Level, 1980–1985 (in Thousands), Cont'd.

	1980	1985	1980–1985	% Change	% Distribution of Increase
First Professional	278	274	(4)	−1.4	−2.7
Public	114	111	(3)	−2.6	−2.0
Private	163	162	(1)	−0.6	−0.7

Private Share of the Enrollment Change:

Total	Increase			85.3
Undergraduate	Increase			70.2
Graduate	Increase			125.7
First Professional	Increase			25.0

E/o Table 8.4
Table 8.5

IS CAPT.

Table 8.5. Composition of the Enrollment Change,
by Level, 1980–1986 (in Thousands).

	1980	1986*	1980–1986	% Change	% Distribution of Increase
Total Enrollment	12,097	12,501	404	3.3	100.0
First-Time Freshmen	2,588	2,214	(374)	−14.5	−92.6
Full-Time	1,749	1,584	(165)	−9.4	−40.8
Part-Time	858	630	(228)	−26.6	−56.4
Other Undergraduate	7,887	8,583	696	8.8	172.3
Total Undergraduate	10,475	10,797	322	3.1	79.7
Men	5,000	5,018	18	0.4	4.5
Full-Time	3,227	3,145	(82)	−2.5	−20.3
Part-Time	1,773	1,873	100	5.6	24.8
Women	5,475	5,779	304	5.6	75.2
Full-Time	3,135	3,203	68	2.2	16.8
Part-Time	2,340	2,576	236	10.1	58.4
Graduate	1,343	1,434	91	6.8	22.5
First Professional	278	269	(9)	−3.2	−2.2
Full-Time Equivalent	8,819	9,059	240	2.7	59.4
Full-Time	7,098	7,219	121	1.7	30.0
Part-Time	4,999	5,325	326	6.5	80.7

NOTE *Preliminary data.

IS CAPT ·

Table 8.6. Composition of the Enrollment Change,
by Age, 1980–1985 (in Thousands).

	1980	1985	1980–1985	% Change	% Distribution of Increase
Total	12,097	12,247	150	1.2	100.0
14–17	247	234	(13)	– 5.3	– 8.7
18–24	7,314	6,915	(399)	– 5.5	– 266.0
25–34	3,114	3,211	97	3.1	64.7
35 +	1,421	1,885	464	32.7	309.3
Men	5,874	5,818	(56)	– 1.0	– 37.3
Total	5,873	5,818	(55)	– 0.9	– 36.7
14–17	99	121	22	22.2	14.7
18–24	3,698	3,494	(204)	– 5.5	– 136.0
25–34	1,569	1,562	(7)	– 0.4	– 4.7
35 +	507	639	132	26.0	88.0
Full-Time	3,689	3,608	(81)	– 2.2	– 54.0
14–17	84	102	18	21.4	12.0
18–24	3,020	2,865	(155)	– 5.1	– 103.3
25–34	508	544	36	7.1	24.0
35 +	77	97	20	26.0	13.3
Part-Time	2,184	2,210	26	1.2	17.3
14–17	15	19	4	26.7	2.7
18–24	677	629	(48)	– 7.1	– 32.0
25–34	1,062	1,020	(42)	– 4.0	– 28.0
35 +	430	542	112	26.0	74.7
Women	6,223	6,429	206	3.3	137.3
Total	6,222	6,429	207	3.3	138.0
14–17	148	113	(35)	– 23.6	– 23.3
18–24	3,616	3,421	(195)	– 5.4	– 130.0
25–34	1,545	1,649	104	6.7	69.3
35 +	914	1,246	332	36.3	221.3
Full-Time	3,408	3,468	60	1.8	40.0
14–17	132	101	(31)	– 23.5	– 20.7
18–24	2,794	2,659	(135)	– 4.8	– 90.0
25–34	367	460	93	25.3	62.0
35 +	115	248	133	115.7	88.7
Part-Time	2,814	2,961	147	5.2	98.0
14–17	17	12	(5)	– 29.4	– 3.3
18–24	821	762	(59)	– 7.2	– 39.3
25–34	1,177	1,189	12	1.0	8.0
35 +	799	998	199	24.9	132.7

E to table 8. 6

Table 8.7. Composition of the Enrollment Change,
by Race, 1980–1986 (in Thousands).

	1980	1986	1980–1986	% Change	% Distribution of Increase
Total Enrollment	12,087	12,501	414	3.4	100.0
White non-Hispanic	9,833	9,915	82	0.8	19.8
Total Minority	1,949	2,242	293	15.0	70.8
Black non-Hispanic	1,107	1,081	(26)	−2.3	−6.3
Hispanic	472	623	151	32.0	36.5
Asian or Pacific Islander	286	448	162	56.6	39.1
American Indian/ Alaskan Native	84	91	7	8.3	1.7
Nonresident Alien	305	344	39	12.8	9.4

ᵃPreliminary data; details may not add to totals because of rounding.
Source: U.S. Department of Education, Center for Education Statistics, 1988.

Table 8.8. Trends in the Population, by Age Group,
1970–2000 (in Thousands).

Year	Total	0–17	18–21	22–24	18–24	25–34	35–64	65+
1970	205,052	69,762	14,718	9,993	24,711	25,323	65,149	20,107
1980	227,658	63,660	17,526	12,814	30,340	37,587	70,365	25,708
1990	249,657	64,337	14,684	11,110	25,794	43,529	84,300	31,697
2000	267,955	67,390	14,612	9,988	24,600	36,415	104,629	34,921
Change:								
1970–80	22,606	(6,102)	2,808	2,821	5,629	12,264	5,216	5,601
1980–90	21,999	677	(2,842)	(1,704)	(4,546)	5,942	13,935	5,989
1990–20	18,298	3,053	(72)	(1,122)	(1,194)	(7,114)	20,329	3,224
% Change:								
1970–80	11.0	−8.7	19.1	28.2	22.8	48.4	8.0	27.9
1980–90	9.7	1.1	−16.2	−13.3	−15.0	15.8	19.8	23.3
1990–20	7.3	4.7	−0.5	−10.1	−4.6	−16.3	24.1	10.2

Sources: U.S. Bureau of the Census, 1982, 1984.

References

U.S. Bureau of the Census. *Preliminary Estimates of the Population of the United States by Age, Sex, and Race: 1970 to 1981.* Current Population Reports, Series P-25, no. 917. Washington, D.C.: U.S. Government Printing Office, 1982.

U.S. Bureau of the Census. *Projections of the Population of the United States by Age, Sex, and Race: 1983 to 2080.* Current Population Reports, Series P-25, no. 952. Washington, D.C.: U.S. Government Printing Office, 1984.

U.S. Department of Education, Center for Education Statistics. *Digest of Education Statistics.* Washington, D.C.: U.S. Government Printing Office, 1988.

E/o Chap. 8

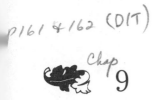

Chap

9

Conclusions and Recommendations: Creating a Brighter Educational Future

by Arthur Levine

In a very real sense, Chapters Two through Six represent a Dickens-like "ghost of Christmas future." They describe what the years ahead hold for colleges and universities, if there are no significant changes within or without. The authors are remarkably consistent in both their analyses and conclusions. Their findings can be divided into four categories: (1) changing population numbers, (2) changing population characteristics, (3) changing populations geographically, and (4) changing patterns of higher education attendance.

Changing Population Numbers

• As is well known, the number of traditional college-age students (eighteen to twenty-two) is declining. Between 1979 and 1986, the numbers dropped steadily for a loss of 21 percent in that age group. This was followed by a slight increase of 7 percent from 1986 to 1989. The largest decrease will occur in the next three years, 1989 to 1992, when the number of eighteen-year-olds will plummet by 17 percent. There will be some relief over the next five years, 1992 to 1997, when there will be a 5 percent recovery. Another 8 percent will be gained by the turn of the century. In short, the next three years will be a very difficult time for higher education as the 1979 population of eighteen-year-olds, 4,451,724, reaches a trough of 3,109,095. This is a decline of nearly one-third of the entire age group.

• At the same time, the number of adults (persons twenty-five and older) will increase for the remainder of the century. However, and this is a very big however, the adult population most likely to attend college will decline. It peaked in 1988 as the baby boomers began sailing into their forties, and it will continue to drop for the rest of the century. Between 1988 and 2000, the pool of adults most likely to enroll in higher education will fall by about 8 percent.

• The one source of students in addition to domestic traditional age and adult populations come from abroad. Immigration seems unlikely to increase, given the political climate in the United States today and the concern with preserving jobs for Americans. Of course, these attitudes could become more fluid in the 1990s if the domestic labor pool fails to keep pace with a growing job market. But while foreign worker programs and increased immigration quotas are certainly possible, colleges and universities should not expect an influx of new immigrant students. Immigrant workers are more likely.

• With regard to foreign students studying in America, trends indicate no large acceleration of numbers, though continuing small gains seem likely.

• In sum, the total population available for higher education can be expected to decline. The next three years could be the most difficult time for colleges and universities in this century, except for the Depression years and the World War II era. The number of eighteen-year-olds will decline sharply, and the large number of adult students who compensated for the loss of traditional students after 1979 will simply not be there. We can expect a decline in the pool of adult students, albeit a gradual one throughout the rest of the century. From now until the year

2000, the college-going population will be smaller than it is currently. In short, colleges can expect enrollment declines of the greatest magnitude through 1992. Enrollments will increase somewhat throughout the rest of the century but will not return to current levels.

Changing Population Characteristics

• The proportion of minorities in the U.S. population is increasing rapidly (see Table 9.1). Between 1979 and 1998, the

IS CAPT.

Table 9.1. Total U.S. Population 1982–2000, by Race (in Millions).

	Total	Black	Hispanic	Asian	White
1982					
Number	232.1	27.7	15.8	3.5	183.5
% of Population	(100.0)	(11.9)	(6.8)	(1.5)	(78.9)
1990					
Number	249.7	31.4	19.9	6.5	192.0
% of Population	(100.0)	(12.4)	(7.9)	(2.6)	(76.8)
% Increase	(7.6)	(13.0)	(26.0)	(86.0)	(0.5)
2000					
Number	268.0	35.8	25.2	10.0	198.9
% of Population	(100.0)	(13.3)	(9.4)	(3.7)	(74.2)
% Increase	(7.3)	(14.0)	(26.0)	(54.0)	(0.4)

R) T

number of white college-aged students will decline by 21 percent, the number of blacks will decrease by 11 percent, the number of Hispanics will increase by 10 percent, and the number of Asians will rise by a substantially greater proportion. This means that the college pool will reflect the increasing minority population to an even larger extent than will the nation as a whole. In fact, by the year 2000, whites will constitute a little over two-thirds of the pool, blacks almost a sixth of the pool, Hispanics nearly a ninth of the pool, and Asians about one-twenty-fifth. Table 9.1

• The groups that are increasing most rapidly in number, with the exception of Asians, are the poorest. Among sixteen-to-twenty-one-year-old whites, one-seventh are living in poverty. This increases for blacks and Hispanics to one-third. Asian rates are comparable to those for whites. However, Asians are a bifurcated group—some of the newer, most quickly growing subgroups, such as the Vietnamese, have poverty rates (35 percent) as high as Puerto Ricans and Mexican Americans, who are the poorest of America's poor. This is unfortunate for higher education because young people who are poor are more likely to have learning disabilities, to fall below grade level and drop out of school, and to experience early pregnancies. In short, they are less likely to attend college than are young persons above the poverty line.

• The fastest growing groups in our population have lower rates of educational attainment. (Once again, Asians are at the extremes.) But this means that future populations are less likely to attend college than were their predecessors (Table 9.2). The rates of college attendance by blacks and Hispanics have actually declined since 1976. The rate for whites is up slightly, and that for Asians is skyrocketing. Table 9.2

Table 9.2. Schooling Completion Rates by Race and Sex
for Persons 25 Years of Age and Older, 1980.

	% High School Graduates		% Completed 4 + Years of College	
	Male	Female	Male	Female
White	69.6	68.1	21.3	13.3
Black	50.8	51.5	8.4	8.3
Hispanic	45.4	42.7	9.4	6.0
Asian	78.8	71.4	39.8	27.0
Chinese	75.2	67.4	43.8	29.5
Vietnamese	71.3	53.6	18.2	7.9

• To summarize, the college-age population will increasingly comprise people of color. The largest of the nonwhite groups—Hispanics and blacks—have the highest rates of poverty and the lowest rates of educational attainment. Their attendance in postsecondary education has been declining for the past decade. Asians are a special group, with wide variations in fertility rates, employment, family income, and educational attainment. What all of this adds up to, however, is that the change in population numbers will be exacerbated by changing population characteristics. Not only is the number of college-age students decreasing, but the groups that make up that population are less likely to attend college. If no preventive action is taken, the decline in college attendance will be even greater than the numbers indicate.

Changing Populations Geographically

• Regionally, every portion of the country is going to experience declines in its college-age population through the early 1990s. The Northeast will have the largest falloff of eighteen-year-olds (30 percent). The Midwest and South will each lose about 20 percent, and the West about 12 percent. The shift in adult students will follow the same pattern.

• Regionally, the Northeast will have the largest proportion of minorities. The South will have the highest percentage of blacks, while the West will have the largest representation of Hispanics and Asians. Hand in hand with these changes is the rising problem of school segregation, worst in the Northeast and South, but bad all over the country.

• Regionally, the Midwest will suffer the largest outmigration of population, and the West will enjoy the greatest increase through immigration.

• By state, the changes will be even more dramatic. Between now and 1992, every state, with nine exceptions, will experience a reduction in the number of high school students that it graduates. More than a third of the states will lose over 10 percent of their students. By the turn of the century, however, all but eleven states can anticipate a return to at least their current graduation rates (Table 9.3). Today there are only thirteen states that can expect to be neither growth areas nor sites of concentration for at least one minority group (Table 9.3).

• Urban areas are becoming crucibles for population changes in size, income level, and race.

Table 9.3. Population Concentration and Growth Areas by State, 1989–2000.

State	Blacks	Hispanics	Asian	American Indian	Immigration	High School Graduates 1986–1992	High School Graduates 1986–2004	College Student Migration
Alabama	+					–		
Alaska				+		+	+	
Arizona	+	+		+		+	+	+
Arkansas	+					–		
California		+	+		+		+	+
Colorado					+	–	+	–
Connecticut						–		–
Delaware						–		
D.C.	+					–		+
Florida	+	+	+		+	+	+	
Georgia	+				+	+	+	
Hawaii			+	+		–		
Idaho						–	–	–
Illinois	+	+	+		+	–	–	+
Indiana						–	–	
Iowa						–	–	
Kansas						–		
Kentucky	+					–		
Louisiana	+					–		
Maine						–		
Maryland	+		+	+	+	–		
Massachusetts			+		+	–		
Michigan	+		+			–	–	

State								
Minnesota				+		−		
Mississippi	+					−	−	
Missouri	+					−		
Montana				+		−	−	
Nebraska						+		
Nevada			+	+	+	−	+	
New Hampshire	+	+				−	+	
New Jersey	+	+	+		+	−		−
New Mexico	+	+				−	+	
New York			+	+	+	−		−
North Carolina				+		−		+
North Dakota				+		−		
Ohio	+		+	+		−		
Oklahoma		+			+	−	+	
Oregon			+	+		−	−	
Pennsylvania			+			−	−	
Rhode Island						−		
South Carolina	+					−		
South Dakota						−		
Tennesee	+		+	+	+	+		
Texas	+		+			+	+	
Utah			+			−	+	
Vermont						−		
Virginia	+		+	+	+	−	+	
Washington					+	−	+	
West Virginia						−	−	
Wisconsin								
Wyoming			+	+			−	

• In conclusion, most areas of the country will experience a loss of population. This loss will be particularly severe during the next three years, diminishing gradually thereafter. The loss will be greatest throughout the old industrial Rust Belt and to a lesser extent in the Midwest and Northeast generally. The Southwest will fare the best, but not uniformly.

Minority populations will vary sharply by region, even by state. For example, Texas, Florida, California, New York, and New Jersey will increasingly become home to all the minority groups that we have discussed. In contrast, very few members of these groups will settle in Delaware, Kansas, and Vermont. Some states will have heavy concentrations of one minority group — Asians in Hawaii, Hispanics in New Mexico, and blacks in Louisiana. But all sorts of other combinations and permutations will occur. What all this means is that higher education in every state will have a unique situation to face. Most of those situations, however, will be less attractive than current ones.

Changing Patterns of Higher Education

• The declining number of young people will put institutions of higher education in the position of having to compete for students with the army, an aggressive labor market, and other noncollegiate postsecondary educators. If these competitors are able to maintain their share of the market, then the decline in college enrollments will be even greater than the numbers and population characteristics now indicate.

• The distribution of colleges and universities nationally is at odds with the geographical changes in population. Institutions of higher education are overrepresented in the areas of largest population declines, that is, the Northeast and Midwest. In greatest jeopardy are small, nonselective, low-endowment, private institutions for traditional-age college students.

• The population changes are not particularly favorable for private colleges and universities in general. They enroll more whites and fewer minorities than the nation's schools as a whole, and so they are reliant on a shrinking portion of the population.

- The future of two-year colleges is uncertain, but troubling. Historically they have been the bellwether of the labor market. When jobs are scarce, their enrollment increases; when jobs are plentiful, their numbers decrease. As employers try to fill positions from a shrinking labor base, community colleges are likely to lose students sooner than other segments of higher education and in the largest numbers.

There are mitigating factors. Two-year colleges have the highest attendance rates by minorities, enrolling them in far higher proportions than any other segment of higher education. Thus, as minority numbers increase, community colleges are likely to be the greatest beneficiary. The opposite is true of adults. As the over-twenty-five college pool declines, two-year institutions that enroll these students in the biggest numbers are likely to be the biggest losers. However, the future of each community college will depend to a large extent on widely varying local population changes.

- Black colleges could be winners. The number of degrees that they awarded fell over the past decade, but the rising proportion of blacks may be sufficient to drive up their enrollments. However, the change in black numbers is relative, not absolute, so the jury is still out.

- Unselective public and private colleges may find themselves hard hit by the game of musical chairs set off by the shrinking college pool. This will be particularly true for nondistinctive institutions in highly competitive locales.

- Selective colleges and universities are facing an enrollment change. Historically, whites have been overrepresented and minorities underrepresented in these institutions. Today they have large numbers of white, Asian, and foreign students but relatively few blacks and Hispanics. Applications to these schools appear to be rising despite population declines and their failure to compensate for the declining pool by admitting adults as many other institutions have done. Asian applications have risen at a startling pace, and, as a result, large questions are being raised about quotas and affirmative action vis-à-vis Asians. Questions are also being raised about the low representation of minorities and the poor in selective colleges and universities.

Such concerns will become increasingly critical as the proportion and number of these populations grow.

• For most colleges and universities, but particularly for public institutions and enrollment-needy private schools, there is likely to be a shift, encouraged both by the states, now increasingly committed to academic accountability and institutional need from the current focus on access to college to a focus on graduation from college. As the populations with the highest attrition rates assume a larger and larger portion of the potential college pool, the issue of retention will greatly increase in importance.

• Similarly, as the pool of students changes, higher education will have to examine the adequacy of the services it offers in such areas as financial aid, academic skills, curricular and co-curricular programming, counseling, faculty and staffing, admissions requirements and transfers, scheduling, and school-college relations, among many others.

• Higher education thus faces much more difficult challenges than it did in the past. Without changes in institutions or the environment, the number of college students will definitely decrease. Institutions will find themselves competing more and more fiercely for this smaller pool of potential students. Nearly all sectors of higher education will be adversely affected, but nonselective public institutions, colleges in the Midwest and Northeast, and private institutions in general will be at greatest risk. The fate of two-year colleges is uncertain, but troubling. And highly selective institutions will be forced to make important changes. Changing populations and numbers will raise a host of new and urgent issues for higher education. These realities point to a period of adversity for colleges and universities as bad as any in the memory of those living today.

What Can Be Done?

This, then, is the future that awaits higher education — unless, that is, something happens to change it. Richard Easterlin and Carol Frances in Chapters Seven and Eight remind us that demographic projections in the past have had a poor track record. They cite a raft of intended and unintended factors, running the gamut from economic conditions and divorce rates to college marketing and high school graduation rates, that have invalidated these projections.

What makes "ghost of Christmas future" projections of this sort important is that they open our eyes. They trot out the most likely tomorrows. They enable us to respond in a number of ways. We can simply wait for the new day to dawn, we can hope that serendipity will intervene in one fashion or another as it usually does to change tomorrow, or we can take action to shape the future in a manner more to our liking.

This volume is written in the belief that trying to shape tomorrow is the best course. There is much that can be done by higher education, government, and the organizations associated with them. Six needs stand out:

1. Redefine the Problem. In looking at the demographic changes ahead, we have seen that the principal conclusion — the bottom line for higher education — is that the number of students will decline. That is the way the problem is almost universally defined, and it is a correct assessment. But it is not the only one.

Indeed, the demographic future might alternately be defined as a problem of underserved populations, that is, a problem involving people who lack educational opportunity, who attend inadequate schools, and who receive too little education. The fact of the matter is that underserved populations can reduce the college pool in precisely the same fashion as a decline in the overall number of students. Actually their effect is far worse.

For example, consider the consequences of focusing on underserved populations for the next ten years. And let us look solely at the effect on eighteen-year-olds. If by 1998, we were able to increase the proportion of blacks and Hispanics graduating from high school to the same rate as whites, this would produce another 158,381 members of the college pool. If by the same year, we were able to raise the college-going rate of blacks and Hispanics to that of whites, this would yield another 159,473 potential students. If the college-going rate of whites who are poor (the bottom two socioeconomic quartiles) could be increased to the average for all whites, this would buoy the pool by 298,155 more members. In combination, these initiatives would produce a total of 616,009 additional eighteen-year-olds for college. And this is just the tip of the iceberg. Enrollments would at the same time rise for those between nineteen and twenty-one, as well as for other age cohorts.

The point is this. The increase in eighteen-year-olds alone would more than compensate for the population decline expected for 1998. In that year, the eighteen-year-old cohort will decrease by 140,821 and the number of adults will fall by 342,000. This totals 482,821 or 28 percent less than the increase in the underserved eighteen-year-old population. Put simply, higher education can more than make up for the demographic decline by better serving the underserved.

The rationales for doing this go far beyond pragmatics. The most basic reason is the American dream. James Agee once wrote, "In every child who is born, no matter what the circumstances and no matter what the parents, the potentiality of the human race is born again" (*Now Let Us Praise Famous Men*, 1939). This is a glorious sentiment. There is no clearer statement of the American dream. Unfortunately, it is not true today for many Americans, and their number has grown larger throughout the 1980s. Restoring the American dream is a national necessity, and today that dream has no more concrete manifestation than attendance at college.

Economic development is a second critical reason for focusing on underserved populations. If the various states are to attract industries and preserve their economic bases, they require an educated labor force. With shrinking numbers of eighteen-year-olds, states are going to desperately need the underserved populations to remain competitive.

Another reason is national defense. America requires a critical mass of people to staff the armed services, to become professionals, to enter careers in science and technology, and to serve as the leaders of tomorrow. With the population declining, the nation needs the currently underserved to take on these roles.

A fourth rationale is social justice. For the most part, the underserved are predominantly people of color and the poor.

They are being discriminated against. That's just not fair, and we used to do better than we are doing now.

Wise investment is a fifth reason. At present, the nation spends money on people after they have suffered all the ill effects of poverty and prejudice. Instead of using tax funds for welfare, prisons, and drug programs, wouldn't it make more sense to invest in people while they are healthy and help them become productive and contributing members of society? In point of fact, it costs less to "invest" in children than in adults, and the payback is higher.

All kinds of other rationales can be offered. But what they add up to is this: Increasing our efforts to assist the underserved will help the underserved, the nation, and higher education too. Everyone will benefit, no one will lose.

A number of initiatives can be recommended to achieve this goal. One of the most badly needed is a government effort which might be called the early childhood intervention program. The educational pipeline is leaking from kindergarten through graduate school. But it is hemorrhaging in its first years. By the time many minority and poor youngsters reach school, it is too late. They are so severely disadvantaged that the schools cannot reach them.

The proposed program might include the following elements. Prenatal and postnatal care are critical for children who are born prematurely with serious, but often avoidable, medical problems. Parenting education with an accent on nutrition is badly needed because parents in the underserved population are often still children themselves and know virtually nothing about diet and child care. Quality local day care is also needed, so that parents can work and provide support for their families. Preschool education for three- and four-year-olds is essential for children born into families with little schooling and low proficiency in English. Such children find themselves far behind their peers when they enter school and never really catch up. Teenage pregnancy prevention is also needed to end the continuing cycle of deprivation in which each pregnancy ensures two generations of poverty — mother and child. And, finally, drug enforcement is key: drugs destroy lives, particularly among education's most underserved.

This is not a program that requires an infusion of new money. It can be carried out by reallocating existing funds. In fact, it might save money by reducing the need for extraordinary medical care and by creating additional taxpayers.

The schools provide a second area for action. The teacher corps needs more instructors from minority groups and more instructors who are fluent in a second language. The number of faculty who speak Asian languages, for example, is woefully inadequate.

Enrollment patterns have to be changed. Our schools are growing increasingly segregated—more and more schools are filled with predominantly underserved populations. According to Lewis Solmon's research, a critical mass of 20 percent increases the likelihood of success for traditionally underserved populations (Chapter Two). But Gary Orfield's data in Chapter Three show clearly that schools with predominantly underserved student bodies are deeply hurtful. Desegregation of our schools is mandatory.

Counseling needs to be improved as well. A large proportion of underserved young people know no one who has ever been to college and few who finished high school. Underserved students need to learn more about the educational process. They need to meet role models—people like themselves who have made it. They need hope and encouragement. They also need better academic guidance. Too many are directed away from the academic track to vocational and general programs that do not lead to college. Too many are directed away from essential courses in math, science, and English that are necessary for advanced study. Social and psychological counseling and support programs are also desperately needed to cope with a myriad of out-of-school problems.

Outreach to parents is also critical. While this can be a difficult and frustrating task, parents must be shown the difference that education can make for them and their children as early as elementary school. They also need to learn about the financial aid that can make this education affordable.

Colleges and universities also have a vital role to play. They need to expand access, and this means that they must use recruiting practices that reach underserved populations. Traditional practices have been notably unsuccessful in this respect. Colleges and universities must design support programs to assist underserved populations — programs that vary from day care and welfare advocacy to residential assistance and job placement offices. They must provide academic programming in skill areas, curricula in fields that touch upon the lives of changing populations, and scheduling consistent with potential student needs. These institutions must hire more faculty from underserved backgrounds and must work as partners with schools from kindergarten through grade 12. There is extensive literature on successful programs in all these areas for schools and colleges that want to act.

Another ingredient is money. In the past, underserved students have followed financial aid to college. During the 1980s, the White House sought to slash student aid, but Congress reduced the magnitude of the proposed cuts. Even so, in real dollars, federal financial assistance has severely declined. The burden has been shifted to the student as loan funds have risen substantially while grants have fallen in equal measure. Both these changes drive underserved students away from higher education. Simply stated, our government policy must change if we are to see our nation's jobs filled and national defense provided for.

Employers can also assist the underserved. Programs that provide students with summer and part-time jobs during the year, financial support for education, role models who visit the schools, and encouragement, hope, and information keep students in school. Industry can make a large contribution here.

2. Make More out of Less. The students who are most likely to graduate from college are, of course, those who are already enrolled in college. Yet less than half graduate within four years, and less than 70 percent graduate from any institution after seven years. The highest dropout rates are for the fastest growing population groups (except in the case of Asians): Asians (17 percent), whites (27 percent), blacks (29 percent), Hispanics (31 percent), and Native Americans (31 percent) (Astin, 1975).

Reducing attrition is the easiest way for colleges to increase their enrollments. It amounts to turning less into more.

Institutions can accomplish this in ways very similar to those used to encourage access. They include

- An institutional commitment to *graduating* students, not simply enrolling them
- Leadership that is knowledgeable about the causes of attrition and the retention methods that work
- An educational program geared to the abilities and needs of the student body and the demands of the economy and society
- A program of easily accessible support services targeted at the particular student body that an institution enrolls
- An attractive, warm, and comfortable environment for students in which relationships with faculty and staff are encouraged
- Outreach into the community and schools in a manner designed to make the college emotionally, physically, and intellectually a part of the community
- A staff that reflects the characteristics of the student body and shares a commitment to their education
- Consistency of financial aid throughout college and a willingness to meet the full financial needs of students

START   Two-year and four-year colleges have a special part to play. The transfer rates from the former to the latter are scandalously low. The highest estimate is that fewer than one-fourth of all community college students ultimately graduate from a four-year school. The gap between the schools is partly cultural, partly attitudinal, partly administrative, partly political, and partly substantive. But there are steps that can be taken to bridge the gap. Simple communication is one. Creating offices on two- and four-year campuses charged with encouraging transfer is helpful. More visits to two-year campuses by four-year staff and students and vice versa make a difference. Faculty exchanges are very valuable, as are close ties between counselors on the different campuses. Clearer articulation statements that detail program and policy agreements are essential. Efforts to cut the red tape of transfer also make it easier to bridge the gap. Continuity in financial aid is a requirement.

However, one of the most helpful actions to enhance retention might come from the federal and state governments. At present, financial aid in the main is tied to enrollment. First-term freshmen and last-term seniors are regarded as interchangeable. It would be useful to develop programs that rewarded graduation and thus provided incentives to colleges and universities to increase the graduation rates of the students they enroll.

3. Improve Sorting. America has built a mass, even universal system of higher education, able to accommodate in excess of 40 percent of all high school graduates. However, the system has been stratified economically and socially since at least the eighteenth century. Its structure underwent various elaborations but was largely completed by the 1920s. Today it consists of two-year colleges at the bottom and highly selective private colleges and research universities at the top. Two-year institutions have a disproportionate number of minority and poor students, while elite colleges and universities have very few students from these populations. Hearn (1984) has shown that lower socioeconomic students and people of color are "less likely to attend more selective institutions" and "less likely to attend higher-resource and higher-cost institutions" (p. 25).

This is not an acceptable situation. It denies opportunity to the fastest growing groups in higher education's pool. It encourages higher attrition rates by clustering the groups with the lowest retention rates in the institutions with the highest attrition rates. It is wrong and it is hurtful.

An important part of the problem is that blacks, Hispanics, and poor people in general score low on traditional tests of academic achievement. If these criteria weigh heavily in college admission — as they do at most highly selective schools — it means that few minorities and poor will qualify for admission.

Recent research by Scott Miller at the Exxon Education Foundation shows the situation to be precisely this. What is needed is a broader net to discover talented students than currently exists. It must be a net that discovers young people very early in their lives by methods other than the familiar standardized tests. We need something similar to the national teacher certification measure currently being developed at Stanford by

Lee Shulman. This could be a wonderful project for one of the many national foundations currently involved in youth, poverty, and minority issues.

A second useful step would be for elite colleges to form partnerships with elementary and junior high schools with the aim of identifying and nurturing bright young people to fill their future classes. High school is too late to begin this process. Similarly, relationships should be established with community colleges, something that is seldom done by elite schools. Two-year colleges possess another pool of talent that is going unharvested.

Beyond this, elite institutions need to expand their admissions standards to increase the enrollment of minorities and the poor. Many colleges have regressed in this respect over the past several years. This situation is not tolerable and invites outside intervention. Several state legislatures are currently debating whether funds should be shifted from elite universities to two-year colleges because of the much larger "bang for the buck," the valued added, that comes from educating the underserved. If elite schools, particularly the public ones, do not get their houses in order, government may well help them in doing so in the years ahead.

Asians are going to be an acid test in making these access barriers public. They are minorities but at the same time are one of the most successful groups in the country in higher education attendance. The soaring number of Asian applications at the best colleges in this country has produced a conflict between the need for affirmative action and the need for diversity. Should Asians be given preference because they are a minority or should their numbers be limited because they are so overrepresented in order to encourage diversity? From California to Massachusetts, this issue is heating up.

The suggestion of those attending the Ford Foundation symposium was that Asians not be treated as a homogeneous group. The most deprived elements, including the Vietnamese, should continue to be given affirmative action treatment. Other groups of Asians that are among the most successful in the country should be treated in a color-blind fashion and be admitted to colleges and universities on the basis of achievement. This division seems more just and appropriate than the all-or-nothing approach usually offered.

    4. Learn from the Past. Colleges and universities had significantly better records in admitting and graduating minorities and the poor in past years. We have lost ground. There has, of course, been much speculation about what changed and why our efforts are less fruitful today. It is now time for research to take us beyond the hypotheses and pet ideological theories.

    Government and foundations could make a large contribution by supporting research on the following questions:

1. Which of the myriad of efforts in the 1960s and 1970s worked and which did not in encouraging minority access and retention?
2. What effect did the decline in civil rights enforcement have upon minority access and graduation rates from schools and colleges? What should be done?
3. What effect have the changes in federal funding formulas had on colleges and their students?
4. What are the model programs that higher education can learn from? Why do they work?
5. What is the effect of inconsistency and changes in policy regarding college admission of minorities and the poor?

The answers to these questions will be very important in guiding future educational policies.

    There is another serious task for the federal government. The data on U.S. population by age, race, geography, socio-economic status, and school attendance are poor. Each of the authors in the volume offered serious criticisms. We lack the data to understand as well as we need to the condition and progress of this nation's various populations. The Department of Education should convene a meeting of the publics for such data, including scholars, policymakers, and practitioners, to determine the deficiencies and needs in existing data and to make improvements in their collection.

    In addition, the government ought to make efforts to consolidate the various demographic data bases from around the country. There are some excellent collections of such data in the private sector — for example, in corporations such as Burger King.

5. *Understand Limitations.* Higher education and government each have inherent limitations that need to be recognized in addressing the demographic future and underserved populations in particular. First, colleges are not the villains. They should not be penalized or criticized for what they have not done. They should be encouraged and rewarded for what they do well. For example, government financial aid ought to provide incentives for colleges with high graduation rates but should not penalize colleges with lesser rates. A negative approach would surely reduce the incentive for admitting higher-risk students and ultimately perhaps reduce college efforts to serve the underserved.

Second, government has limited resources. Education must not be greedy in seeking public funds. Higher education should take the lead in designing and implementing programs to serve the underserved. Government should vigorously support colleges and universities in these efforts. It should work with higher education rather than seek to impose solutions upon it. Government might encourage colleges through the use of competitions and requests for proposals to develop models and innovative approaches for serving the underserved. This has worked excellently in New Jersey. And the resources for these solutions must be committed for the long run, not the quick fix.

6. *Recognize That Each College and University Can Determine Its Own Future.* This goes without saying. Every college in America is facing a somewhat different set of demographic circumstances. Each has the ability to do nothing, to hope for serendipity, or to shape tomorrow. The choice is entirely theirs.

References

Astin, A. W. *Preventing Students from Dropping Out.* San Francisco: Jossey-Bass, 1975.

Hearn, J. S. "Socioeconomic Characteristics in College Destination." *Sociology of Education,* 1984, 57, 22–30.

Index